PLUGGING IN PARENTS

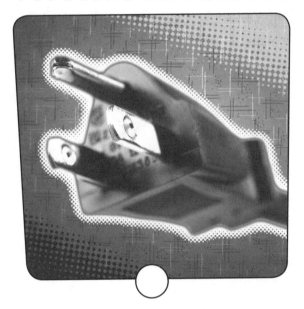

200 WAYS TO INVOLVE PARENTS
IN YOUTH MINISTRY

D1418249

Group

Loveland, Colorado

PLUGGING IN PARENTS
200 WAYS TO INVOLVE PARENTS IN YOUTH MINISTRY

Credits

Contributing Authors: Steve Argue, Jenny Baker, Rick Beno, Jim Burns Mark DeVries, Joel Fay, Kurt Johnston, Mikal Keefer, Joy-Elizabeth F. Lawrence, Rick Lawrence, Dave Livermore, Jeanne Mayo, Michael McConnell, James W. Miller, Walt Mueller, Julia L. Roller, Christina Schofield, Thom and Joani Schultz, Amy Simpson

Acquisitions Editor: Kelli B. Trujillo   Editor: Lyndsay E. Gerwing
Chief Creative Officer: Joani Schultz   Copy Editor: Deborah Helmers
Art Director: Toolbox Creative   Designer/Illustrator: Toolbox Creative
Cover Art Director: Jeff Storm   Cover Designer: Susan Tripp
Cover Photographer: Rodney Stewart   Production Manager: Dodie Tipton

Special thanks to Tony Akers, Rik Alspaw, Kevin Antrim, Jamie Aten, Tom Atkinson, Darrell Back, Jim Beckner, Vanessa Berger, Gary Bodford, Jodi Boom, Louise Boom, Robyn Carnes, David Chow, Rick Chromey, Tony Dennis, Daniel DeVore, Eric Geiger, Rachel Gilmore, Eric Gledhill, Rob Goff, Jennifer Hale, Terrance Hale, Michael Harder, Matt Harris, Holly Henningfeld, Natalie Hokanson, Tricia Johnson, Nathan Kilgore, Chad Kimberley, Neal Kloster, Donny Kyker, Jay Lehman, Gary Long, Janis Long, Jeremy Marburger, Mike McNeill, Steve Merritt, Pat Meyer, Jason Mitchell, Kym Mitchell, Julie Montgomery, Drew Moser, Joe Neary, Christin O'Neill, Gene Ramsey, Justin Raulston, Gary Ridge, Courtney Roes, Mark Schaufler, Robert Schaut, Andy Shannon, Dale Sheehy, Bronwyn Skov, Todd Slocum, Jo Ann Smith, Tom Stephen, David Stevenson, Michael Stone, Rachel Sullivan, Walter Surdacki, Paul Talley, Susan Tanigawa, Brian Telzerow, Helen Turnbull-Goody, Michelle VanderWal, James Vink, Jon Waind, Kim Wills, and Phil Wilson for their contributions to the Group Magazine ideas used in this book.

Library of Congress Cataloging-in-Publication Data

Plugging in parents : 200 ways to involve parents in youth ministry.
  p. cm.
  ISBN 0-7644-2822-5 (pbk. : alk. paper)
  1. Church work with youth. 2. Parent and teenager. 3. Christian education of teenagers. I. Group Publishing.
  BV4447.P554 2005
  259'.23—dc22   2005005024

10 9 8 7 6 5 4 3 2 1   14 13 12 11 10 09 08 07 06 05

Printed in the United States of America.

TABLE OF CONTENTS

INTRODUCTION

What's the most important part of a youth program? Well, it wouldn't be a youth program without the youth. The youth pastor is definitely important. Volunteers are pretty necessary. So what are we forgetting?

Oh, yeah—the parents.

Parental support (or lack thereof) can make or break your youth program. And since parents are the number one most important ingredient in developing their teenagers' faith, *connecting* with parents is the ultimate way to help teenagers grow in faith.

Parents need to be kept up to date on what's going on in your youth group. They need to know with whom their teenagers are spending time and whether or not that time is well-spent. And, believe it or not, parents also need spiritual support and prayer. The best way to do these things is to *involve* parents in every aspect of your ministry to youth, from volunteering to praying to taking the message home in devotions and activities.

Parents raising teenagers probably already feel very plugged in to conflict. Their kids disagree with them on a regular basis. Parents know conflict is natural, but they still find their world rocked when a child who once considered them the center of the universe snarls and says, "I hate you."

Conflict may be uncomfortable, but it *is* communication. And it *is* an opportunity for plugging in to the lives of your kids' families…and plugging those parents in to your ministry.

Plugging In Parents addresses the number one complaint in youth ministry: parents. It will help you learn ways to respect parents, love them, and connect with them!

Plugging In Parents includes 200 fun, creative ways to connect parents with your youth ministry. Fresh, practical ideas are organized in helpful sections to help you successfully connect with parents. And connecting with parents brings tremendous benefit to your youth ministry because caring for parents results in spiritual growth for students!

Find the hidden talents of the parents in your group.

1

INVOLVING PARENTS IN PLANNING AND VOLUNTEERING

VOLUNTEER PLEDGE DRIVE

Parents need to feel informed about the ministry to which they are entrusting their kids. One effective method of spreading information and generating excitement is to hold annual banquets. These banquets can range from fund-raisers to appreciation nights to game nights. Whatever the purpose, try to take advantage of these times by making them volunteer-recruitment opportunities.

Simply share how God is using your church's ministry to change lives. Then hold a pledge drive for volunteer contributions. Instead of asking for money, ask for time, prayer commitments, and administrative support. During this time, present the calendar of events for the next six or 12 months. Have students talk about the impact the youth ministry has made on their lives. Show videos of past events.

Talk about what kind of volunteer help you require to do all the cool stuff you have planned for the future. Break everything down into a variety of specific needs. That way, people can volunteer for short-term or even one-time tasks rather than feeling like they have to hang out with teenagers 24/7 if they want to help. Let people sign up for what they'll pledge to do to keep the ministry going.

Then be sure to hold people to the commitments they make. In fact, one of the parents might be perfectly suited to contact others and remind them of what they have committed to do.

MONEY TALKS

Money makes a difference—even to volunteers!

When you organize events that cost money, put out the word that you'll give a discount to students whose parents help with the event. This makes an especially significant difference to parents who have more than one student attending such events. They may become your most dependable volunteers!

So what about the events that don't cost money? When parents help with free events, allow them to earn scholarship "credit" toward future events that do cost. That way their teenagers can receive discounts in the future.

Be sure your discounts aren't so large that they'll break your church budget, but do make the discounts significant enough that they'll make a difference to parents. Make sure that you have an organized system for keeping track of the credits people earn toward future discounts and that you keep your records up to date. Parents won't want to participate unless they know you're dependable in giving them what they've earned.

IF YOU WERE THE YOUTH WORKER...

Have parents fill out a survey (the best methods of distribution are giving it out by hand at a parent meeting, e-mailing it, and posting it on your church's Web site—and, yes, you should do all three). The primary purpose of the survey is not to solicit volunteers but to ask for feedback on the program. Introduce the survey at the top with the words "Your feedback is important to us."

Ask parents anything that might be helpful for improving the student ministry: what they would like to see their teenagers gain from the program, what their experience of church was like as a teenager, whether times and costs of your programs are reasonable to them, what they would change, and so on. To gain specificity, offer a list of things that you do and ask for comments on each one, such as weekly meetings, retreats, and overnighters.

Using their responses, try to identify a key issue for each parent, what he or she most appreciates or is most concerned about. Then call that parent to ask if he or she would help you with that particular need. You've already eliminated a primary obstacle to recruiting volunteers: You're helping them find a cause that they feel passionate about.

CAN YOUR PET DO THIS?

Every youth group needs a good PET (Parent E-visory Team). What can this PET do? An electronic advisory team can get feedback to a youth leader quickly and effectively. Here is a simple process with inclusive thinking and powerful potential.

This e-visory idea utilizes e-mail to involve parents in important decision making. Solicit parents to become members of the youth group PET. Using a name like PET, you may present the subject very creatively.

Youth leaders always need good advice and direction. Decisions made with parental support are better poised to succeed. With a PET e-mail list, incorporating these benefits is only a mouse-click away. In order to manage the process, give your PET a specific calling. Consider using your PET for e-vice on the following subjects:

- Event planning
- Staffing decisions
- Conflict resolution
- Administrative complexities
- Fund raising

Utilizing a PET empowers youth leaders, integrates parents, and encourages youth. Best of all, this PET doesn't need feeding, walking, or grooming. See what your PET can do for you.

PROACTIVE VOLUNTEER RECRUITMENT!

When Jesus met the woman at the well, he asked her for some water. He deliberately chose to put himself in her debt; he needed something from her. And what followed was an amazingly deep conversation about spiritual things (John 4).

So next time you need some help from parents, follow Jesus' example. Instead of waiting for them to volunteer to help you out, call them on the phone or send them a note or an e-mail and ask them if they can help with specific tasks. You may feel awkward about asking, but there's no need to! People will say no if they are too busy or can't help for some reason, but most will be pleased to play their part. Although parents will hear general appeals for volunteers, many people just don't get around to thinking about how they could fulfill the need. Asking for help is a great way to start a relationship with someone and shows that you need and expect his or her involvement. If you don't know the parents very well, choose something simple that's not too time-consuming. Make sure you approach everyone in rotation—if you don't need them all for this activity, save some for the next!

TALENT SPOTTING

Find out the hidden talents and skills of the parents in your group, and make a point of using them in your program. For example, if someone is good at hospitality, have the youth barbecue at that person's house instead of thinking you have to play host all the time. If someone is great at desktop publishing, get him or her to design a newsletter or publicity. If someone is a Trekkie (*Star Trek* fan), tell that person what topics you're going to be teaching and ask him or her to go through episodes on video and find clips you can use.

You could send out a form for parents to fill out at the start of the school year, asking if they have anything they could contribute to the youth program, but you'll need to play detective as well! When you talk to parents, listen for things they're enthusiastic about.

Ask your church leader if he or she has any suggestions for specific contri-

butions parents might be able to make. When members of your group talk about what their families have been doing, make a mental note of any things they might contribute. Having accumulated your list of parental talents, think about ways in which you might be able to incorporate these into the program, even if it means trying something new. We all like to feel that we are wanted and needed, so asking parents to contribute what they are good at is a winner all around!

SOUL FOOD

Enlist parents' help to feed hungry teenagers at your meetings. Some zealous parents may even be willing to host the crew on occasion.

Advertise your need in the church newsletter and bulletin, and place a sign-up sheet on a bulletin board in a heavily trafficked hall of the church. When the list is full, have students help you organize a food calendar.

Use recipe cards to write reminder postcards to those parents who have offered to serve. Include the meeting date parents should provide for, and include instructions about where they should drop off the snacks.

Don't forget to thank them for their labor of tastiness.

DRIVERS' EDUCATION II

What kills teenage drivers isn't just a lack of experience; it's attitude, too. And while drivers' education programs are a great place to instill solid skills, attitude adjustments are best achieved outside the classroom.

Several dads in a Colorado church discovered that their children were getting learner's permits at about the same time. After commiserating for a few weeks about their new drivers' impatience and aggressive driving, the dads decided to help shape their kids' attitudes.

A father who worked as an insurance agent arranged a field trip to a garage, where a somber group saw firsthand what impatience can do to sheet metal. The Bible study about self-control that followed had a significant impact.

Another dad introduced the new drivers to a family whose car had been hit by a careless driver. The family's scars were still visible and led to a great discussion about responsibility and caring for others.

What would it take for you to find several volunteers to organize field trips and Bible studies around a landmark transition like getting a driver's license, entering high school, or getting ready for a prom?

MOVING PARENTS OFF THE BENCH

I have a confession to make. Until recently, I suffered from a strange malady not uncommon to youth workers: parentophobia. I loved teenagers with a passion, but I feared their parents. And because of my fears, I avoided parents and failed to involve them in my youth ministry.

Eventually I admitted my awkwardness and discomfort to a volunteer who'd asked me why I always relied on her to communicate with the parents. Her insight helped me realize that I was suffering from parentophobia.

Since I'm now working my 12-step parentophobia program, I've come to realize the enormous benefit of including parents in my ministry. Not having parents involved was like trying to play basketball with only half a team.

Tipoff

First, I had to make a commitment to involve parents. Then I had to make an effort to get to know them. To move beyond casual chitchat, I did simple things such as connecting with them at church to ask how things were going and whether there was any way I could help them. At our quarterly parents meetings, I took time during and after the meetings to find out what challenges they were facing.

Whenever I called a young person at home, I'd take a few extra minutes to talk to the parent who answered the phone. I began inviting parents to lunch and tried to get myself invited to dinner (this works great if you're single and you can't cook).

Game Plan

Once parents realized that I cared about them, I discovered they were very willing to help out in various ways, such as offering their homes, assisting at meetings, leading small groups, serving as camp counselors, and providing needed resources. One slice of wisdom: If you're going to ask parents to contribute their time, make sure you ask them well in advance. Asking parents to help out two days before your event doesn't exactly make you look very organized or professional.

HOW NOT TO GET PARENTS OFF THE BENCH

While it's easy for us as youth workers to blame parents for their lack of interest in our ministry, we need to accept our own responsibility. Often we do things, intentionally and unintentionally, that discourage parents from getting involved. Here's a list of the top 10 parent turnoffs:

10. Forget to plan or think ahead. Call parents at the last minute for help, and don't give them an opportunity to say no.

9. Forget to say "please" when asking parents for help and "thank you" when they do.

8. Use only college-age volunteers in your youth ministry. Assume parents' wisdom and experience don't mean anything in youth ministry.

7. Give in to your parentophobia. Convince yourself and your staff that avoiding parents is good youth ministry.

6. Keep everything a secret from parents. Make everything a surprise and just expect parents to "trust you."

5. Ask only churched parents to help in the youth ministry. Believe that unchurched parents don't want to help and that God can't possibly reach them through your youth ministry.

4. Communicate that you know what it's like to parent a teenager. Convey to parents that they don't know what they're doing, and present yourself as the expert on teenagers. Let parents know that if they just follow your 10 easy steps to parenting teenagers, they can be just like you.

3. Assume that you love your group members more than their parents do.

2. Take full responsibility for the spiritual nurture of teenagers. Communicate to parents that it's not their responsibility to raise their children in the Lord. Expect them to disregard Bible passages such as Psalm 78:1-7; Deuteronomy 6:4-9; Proverbs 22:6; and Ephesians 6:4.

1. Refuse to admit you are wrong, and fail to learn from your mistakes.

(Adapted from Group Magazine, January/February 2001)

Another way I involve parents is by sharing information with them. If what we do in youth group is a mystery to parents, they're left with the task of trying to find out from their teenagers what's going on. And usually what comes out of their teenagers' mouths is "nothing." Communicating the purpose of programs and events goes a long way to help keep parents committed. When parents understand the "why" behind what we're doing, they're much more willing to be supportive.

For example, every fall we do a major all-night outreach event. When I clearly explain that the purpose of the all-nighter is to reach unchurched teenagers, parents are a lot more accepting of their teenagers' participation—and more willing to lend a hand. Letting parents know what topics you're teaching, and mailing or sending home parent-teen discussion sheets also helps connect parents to your youth ministry.

When I include parents in key ministry decisions, such as whether to change an existing program, start a new one, or pull the plug on an old one, parents not only feel involved but also support the outcome.

Another winning strategy is to engage parents in ministry to other parents. Through our parent ministry team, we've offered seminars and Bible studies for parents and created a parent resource library and a parent newsletter. While I give leadership to the team, it's the parents who are the backbone. This allows me to increase my impact with parents without adding to my schedule.

Score!

Getting parents off the bench and into the game is no easy task, but it's definitely a worthwhile goal: You and kids' parents will have cause to celebrate—and the biggest winners of all will be the young people in your youth ministry.

(Adapted from Group Magazine, January/February 2001)

THE PARENT TRAP

I know what you complained about last night. I can just see you standing in your kitchen unloading the day on your spouse or roommate. There you are, gritting your teeth as you line up some kid's parent in your cross hairs.

When Group Magazine asked youth leaders around the world what they complain about most, "lack of parental involvement" squashed all the other responses by an Olympic mile.

Here's the rogues' gallery of youth ministers' top beefs:
- Lack of parental involvement
- Bad attitudes
- Your pastor
- Too busy
- Volunteers
- Salary
- Other church staffers
- The church bus

Youth leaders have always had a love-hate relationship with their group members' parents, but a lot of you are downright infuriated with them—all the time. What's going on here?

Much has been written in Group Magazine's Trends section about the whys and hows of parents' diminishing involvement in their kids' lives. One factor is that there are more dual-income and single-parent families than before, and that's put the squeeze on parents' time. Unfortunately, one casualty of that time squeeze is the relationships parents have with their teenagers. On average, parents spend just 14 minutes per day with their teenagers. Small wonder, then, that 20 percent of teenagers identify "not enough time with my parents" as their top concern in life.

So what's the cure? First, we have to step over a big hurdle called anger. You're a youth minister because you love teenagers and are passionate about helping them grow in Christ. And you're continually frustrated in your attempts to convince the most important people in your kids' lives to give them their most precious resource—time. Mix these things together and you get anger. And you'll never make headway with parents when they know you're angry with them. So try something they'd never expect—be their most vigorous supporter.

Don't compete with them. Parents are looking to the church to be an ally in raising their children, not a competitor. Ask your kids' parents how your program helps and hurts their family's growth and togetherness. Strengthen what helps; prune what doesn't.

Go the extra mile. If you don't send out a parent newsletter, get started. If one parent meeting time is inconvenient for half of your parents, plan a second time. If you've asked a parent three times for help and heard "no" each time, risk a fourth no.

Publicly praise powerful parenting. Whenever you can, wherever you can, sniff out the great things your kids' parents are doing and make a big deal about them.

Make it easy for them to get involved. When your kids are raising money for a mission trip, raise a little more and make it free for parents to come along.

Anyone can get angry—it takes courage to be generous to a fault.

(Adapted from Group Magazine, November/December 2000)

PIE AUCTION

Dig in to a tasty and lucrative fund-raising favorite! Ask your teenagers and their parents to provide pies for sale. Publicize your auction, and hold it one hour before a regularly held meeting, such as a quarterly congregational meeting or a volunteer recruiting meeting, or after a midweek worship service.

Recruit a local auctioneer to emcee the pie auction. Have your youth group members serve ice cream, lemonade, and coffee to guests as they arrive.

To present the items for auction, ask a teenager or youth group sponsor to hold up a pie while other teenagers record the bids. Encourage your youth group members to pool their money and bid against the adults. When the youth group wins a pie, have everyone grab a fork and dig right in!

(Adapted from Group Magazine, September/October 2004)

HEART

To involve more adults with your youth group activities, create a special HEART—Helpful and Enthusiastic Adult Reinforcement Team.

Every other month, send all the parents and adults in your church personal invitations to a HEART meeting. At this meeting, have teenagers and adults who develop your programming give reports describing recent and upcoming events and then offer volunteer opportunities. These should be limited commitments that might include providing transportation for a sporting event, providing a snack for a weekly meeting, or co-leading a Bible study. Circulate sign-up sheets, and you may be surprised to find them filled! Limit the meetings to one hour, and serve refreshments.

(Adapted from Group Magazine, September/October 2004)

THREE DEGREES OF INVOLVEMENT

Give parents choices for their levels of commitment in volunteering in youth ministry. You could define volunteer opportunities for the parents of youth group members as follows:

- Available—This level of parent leadership is perfect for parents who don't want too much involvement or aren't able to commit to a lot of time. However, they can help in one of the following ways: drive; set up or clean up at events; provide props, security, or access to pools and clubs; or open their homes for youth group activities. These leaders help throughout the year at a number of events.
- Involved—These parents are involved in a specific area of youth ministry, usually on a monthly basis. They rotate into Sunday morning or Wednesday night schedules or possibly a bimonthly Bible study.
- Committed—This leadership opportunity is for those committed to weekly ministry. It's filled with parents who want to have a role in the spiritual development of students. Involvement at this level requires an application process. Parents attend monthly meetings and make a school-year-long commitment to one of the ongoing ministries.

(Adapted from Group Magazine, January/February 2004)

COUPLE UP

If your youth ministry is blessed with highly motivated parents, here's a novel recruitment plan that will help you draw in parents to serve as adult leaders.

Depending on the size of your youth group, recruit a number of couples who agree to serve for a set amount of time. To set this plan in motion, recruit half the initial couples to serve for one year and half to serve for two years.

At the end of the first year, have the couples who are staying recruit new couples (with input from the teenagers) who will work with them for the following year. As the plan goes forward, these additional couples will also serve for two years, and after their first year, they'll recruit new couples.

The new couples coming in each year will bring freshness, and the couples who have already served for one year will bring continuity and experience.

(Adapted from Group Magazine, May/June 2003)

JUST-RIGHT COMMITMENTS

Don't limit adult leaders to a one-size-fits-all commitment. Instead, identify varying degrees of involvement. Here's how one veteran youth pastor defines four levels of service:

- Friends—Ministry friends are those who have a general concern for the youth ministry but aren't able to assist with ongoing ministries. They're often able to serve as advocates on church boards, and they occasionally help during youth ministry events.
- Chaperones—These are event-based, on-call volunteers with a willingness to show up as drivers or as extra help for events, trips, and retreats.
- Sponsors—As youth ministry regulars, sponsors are present at most youth ministry functions. They're genuinely concerned about the students and assist with the practical concerns of the youth ministry. They may provide snacks, write encouraging letters, make phone calls, and show up for games, recitals, and other school events.
- Counselors—These well-trained, highly committed team members participate in all youth ministry events and are assigned a number of young people for pastoral care. Counselors act as small group leaders, teachers, and Bible study leaders. Pastors at heart, they're often the ones who stay after youth group to talk and pray with teenagers.

(Adapted from Group Magazine, January/February 2003)

YOUTH BOOSTERS

If you have a capable staff that can make sound youth ministry decisions but you lack support for big events and special projects, recruit a "second-tier" team of Youth Boosters.

Have this group of parents and adults meet only as needed. Keep the meetings short, upbeat, and focused on a specific event. Possible tasks include assisting with mailings and phone calls to make sure young people have information regarding the event. Boosters can also follow through on other tangible needs, such as shopping, cooking, setting up, driving, or making deliveries.

(Adapted from Group Magazine, March/April 2003)

PARENTS INC.

If your ministry would profit from the involvement of more parents, make them an offer to invest not money but time in a venture that's guaranteed to bring rewards.

Create a fancy brochure to advertise your new "corporation," Parents Inc. Include your bylaws, strategies, and youth ministry philosophy. Offer every parent the chance to be on the "board of directors" if he or she is willing to invest two hours a month for a Sunday afternoon meeting and one night a month to help with a youth activity.

At the monthly meeting, have parents brainstorm activities for the following month and enlist volunteers to help. Some types of involvement might be providing food for the large-group meeting; opening their homes for Bible studies, video nights, or holiday parties; taking a three-hour shift during a lock-in; or shuttling kids to and from events. Also, invite a teenager to attend the meeting and tell parents something about what God has been doing in his or her life through the youth ministry.

When parents see that their ideas are being used to reach young people for Christ, they'll be much more likely to give their time and resources to help the youth ministry succeed.

(Adapted from Group Magazine, July/August 2002)

By recruiting six parents to serve as parent advisers, you can stay informed about the needs of the families connected to your youth group.

Meeting with a few parents can be a lot easier than meeting with all the parents. Bounce your dreams and ideas off your parent council, and challenge them to keep you accountable to a family-ministry perspective.

If you make sure the parents on your council are well-informed and effectively used, they'll become strong supporters of your ministry. They'll know just what topics are most important to the other parents, and in time they'll be capable of organizing and running your quarterly parent meetings. You may even gain six more drivers for the next road trip.

(Adapted from Group Magazine, May/June 2001)

CONFESSIONS OF A NON-INVOLVED PARENT
By Mikal Keefer

Well, it's happened: I've become one of those "non-involved" parents I found so frustrating when I was a youth leader.

You know our type: Our kids are plugged in to youth group—at the weekly meetings; on the worship team; at every retreat, workcamp, and service project—but we never get involved ourselves.

You see us drop off kids in the parking lot and see our names on checks to cover concert tickets…but that's it.

What is *wrong* with us? When the youth program gives our kids so much, why aren't we in there helping?

Fair question.

And here's my answer: My kids told me I'm not *allowed* to participate. When it comes to youth group, I've been banned. I'm in permanent timeout. Persona non grata.

Don't believe me? Ask them.

Listen, if you don't have teenagers of your own, you might not understand this, but some of your kids view youth group as theirs and theirs alone. They don't want Mom or Dad inside a hundred *miles* of meetings.

So that's something you should know about me (and some of your kids' parents): I'm a *reluctant* no-show. I'd be more involved if I could be—but I want my son and daughter to stay connected to the group. If that means I have to stay away, I'll do it.

But if you'll suggest a volunteer job that doesn't involve being at the meetings, I'm your guy. I'll organize a fund-raiser. I'll do the newsletter. I'll make phone calls. I want to help—just not in person.

While we're at it, let me tell you a couple of other things about me. I'm betting they're true of many of your kids' parents, too.

I appreciate you.

Hey, I remember all-night lock-ins. That you're willing to host one for my kids… well, I know it costs you something. Thanks for providing memorable events for my children. Thanks for being a safe adult who influences my son and daughter for the kingdom.

Don't assume my lack of involvement signals a lack of appreciation.

I want to treat you like a professional.

Believe it or not, even though we don't look alike or listen to the same music, I respect your ministry role. If I haven't said that enough, forgive me.

And yet the communication that works so well with my kids doesn't connect with me. It's great that you're an awesome worship leader, but I want to know the programming goals for next quarter. I want to know if it's worth giving up a family camping trip so my kids can go to the music festival.

It's asking a lot, but I expect you to be able to talk to multiple constituencies…and I'm one of them. My daughter is wowed when you pull out a guitar. I'm wowed when you pull out a planning calendar and show me what's coming up three months in advance.

You do a great job speaking my kids' language. Speak mine, too.

I want to be invited to talk with you.

You always hear from the parents who have complaints, so it's easy for you to start dreading phone calls—or ducking them. But I want to know I can talk with you and share my concerns—and my praises. If you don't invite comments, I'm unsure how to give them to you.

When's the last time you held a conference night, like the schools have? You schedule one, and I'll be there to talk about the spiritual development of my children.

Which leads me to mention…

I know I'm accountable for my children's spiritual development —and you aren't.

True, you have influence—lots of it. But for better or worse, I'm the one who'll shape my kids most. I'm the person Scripture charges with raising my children to know, love, and follow God.

I see you as a teammate in the process, but you're not in charge of it. I am. That's why I want to know what you're doing, and why. That's why it's important that you let me know what you're doing in the youth program.

And when it comes to communicating with me, please remember…

My kids don't tell me squat.

OK, you reminded my daughter four times that the fall retreat date was moved up a week. You sent out three e-mails to the kids. Maybe you even posted the info on the youth group Web site.

I still didn't know.

Smoke signals are a more reliable communication channel than teenagers. Telling my kids something you want me to know is usually futile. Talk with me directly—I want to hear from you.

I want my kids to talk with you…sort of.

I recall how critical I was as a teenager. I remember zeroing in on the hypocrisy of my parents, their failings, the shortcomings of our family.

I suspect you'll hear about the dirty laundry too. You won't get a balanced view of our family, and truth be told, I wonder if you're hearing things I wish I could refute, things that are unfair or so heavily filtered that they're untrue.

Yet I want my kids to confide in you. I want them to have a safe place to vent.

I just want to be reassured you'll handle it appropriately.

Sometimes I'm jealous of you.

I can tell my daughter something 300 times and it bounces off. But you mention it once at a retreat and she takes it to heart.

And I'm the one who pays for her braces, patches up her hurts, and listens when she talks nonstop about her best friend, her second-best friend, and the friend who *used* to be her best friend. So why are you her favorite grown-up?

You have a voice into my little girl's life. I don't know if you realize how powerful that is, what a gift you've been given.

Use it wisely.

Let God speak through you.

Mikal Keefer is the father of a teenage son and pre-teenage daughter, and he is a former children's and youth worker. He writes frequently for youth ministry resources.

ENLISTING PARENTS
AS PRAYER SUPPORTERS

ADOPT A FAMILY

Host a family prayer night for your students' families. At the prayer event, spend plenty of time praying together, in family groups and in mixed small groups. Lead the families in praying for themselves, each other, the church, the nation, and the world.

Along with spending time in prayer, allow some time for families to get to know one another. Introduce each family, and give plenty of opportunity for sharing prayer needs.

At the end of the event, ask each family to put its name on a slip of paper. Collect the slips, put them in a bowl, and have each family draw a name, making sure no family gets its own name. Tell families they're adopting each other as prayer partners. The name each family drew is the name of the family it will pray for on a regular basis over the next month.

Before families leave, make sure they all know who their partner families are. Then follow up with families during the next week to be sure they're following through on their commitments to pray for each other.

Encourage these partner families to get together and keep each other updated with prayer needs. At the end of the month, get the families together again to pray and talk about how they ministered to each other. Then if you want to, have them draw names again!

ADOPT A YOUTH

During a series on prayer, request that students volunteer to be "prayer adopted" by other Christians in the body of Christ. Explain that the body of Christ is to uplift and encourage one another no matter what our differences may be.

Explain that the youth group is going to begin a campaign with youth group parents so they can "Adopt a Youth" for prayer. Individuals and families who have a passion for prayer will sign up and commit to praying for a specific person for a specific amount of time. The students' prayer partners will contact them weekly and ask how they would like to be prayed for.

Have willing students fill out information cards that will inform their new prayer partners who they are, what year they are in school, what their favorite hobbies are, what energizes them, what scares them, how they are struggling (whatever they're comfortable sharing), and any other information you may find pertinent.

Give the cards to parents who want to participate in this program. Have the parents call their assigned students weekly and e-mail you to confirm that they made phone contact. You can continue this program as long as it's effective.

PRAYING PARENTS

If you want to enlist parents as prayer supporters for your ministry, why not give them an official volunteer role to do just that?

Create an official volunteer position, "Praying Parent." Advertise your need for parents to fill this role, and create a job description for the volunteers. Take on as many people as want to volunteer in this way. You may find that a lot of parents have been filling this role already, without the official volunteer position.

Once you have your volunteers, enlist a teenager to collect the prayer requests students share during your meetings. This teenager should be responsible and mature and should have some discernment to know when it's important to protect the privacy of students who share requests. You may even want to have the teenager submit the list of requests to you before it goes anywhere else.

Once the list is ready, ask the teenager to send the prayer requests from the group via e-mail to the people on the "Praying Parent" team once a week. Then be sure to remember to keep the team updated on the answers to prayer!

PRAY DAY

One common but effective way of enlisting parents as prayer supporters is to send out a monthly calendar. List a student's name on each day, and encourage parents to pray for that student on that day. You can also list youth events, birthdays, and other important dates on the calendar.

Consider these other prayer calendar ideas to help get parents praying:

- Instead of listing student names on each day, list a family name. On that day, the listed family can pray for the youth ministry, the kids, and the youth leaders.
- Ask parents to call or send a note to the students they are praying for on the day they pray.
- Have students write short prayer requests that can be included with their names on their days.
- Along with student names on each day, print a small thumbnail picture of the student in the calendar box for that day.
- Instead of listing a student on each day, list a student for each week.
- During youth meetings, pray for the students on the prayer calendar for that week.
- List the students to be prayed for that week in your church bulletin, and encourage both parents and nonparents to pray.

A LOT IS RIDING ON OUR TIRES

Before you go on a retreat or mission trip, invite parents to sign up to pray for students other than their own. Ask the parents to each write a letter to the teenagers before you leave to be given to the youth during the trip. It should be a simple note of encouragement, letting the student know that the parent is praying for him or her. It might tell how important the youth group can be to the teenager. Make sure all parents know you're not asking for gifts so that all students receive the same thing. In exchange, give the parents a printed list of things they could pray for each day that you are gone (safety, spiritual growth, sleep!).

During the trip, don't just hand out the cards; take a special moment to explain to the students what you've done as you distribute them. Let them know that the church is like a family and truly cares for them.

The end result is that not only is someone praying for your students but you create a stronger connection between the youth group and your congregation.

YOU'VE GOT PRAYERS

E-mail is a powerful tool for communication in our modern society. Add this power to charge up the prayer lives of your youth and their parents.

Use e-mail to distribute prayer requests to youth group parents. Parents will have a wonderful opportunity to reply with prayers for the group. These prayers will be communicated to the group, and everyone will be drawn closer to each other and the Lord who hears them.

On a weekly basis, give each teenager a blank index card and a pencil or pen. Encourage the youth to write any prayer requests they have. Enter the prayer requests into an e-mail, and send it out to the parents. The e-mail will ask the parents to reply with a written prayer to address the prayer requests.

When you receive the replies, cut and paste the parental prayers into a creatively designed document. Then read the prayers to the youth group at the next weekly meeting. The prayer document can be given to the youth and displayed somewhere in the meeting room or church. It will be like a divine voice declaring, "You've got prayers!"

PRAYING WITH A PROP

Parents of younger children are very familiar with all their children's possessions, but as children get older, they begin to accumulate things the parents are unaware of. Have parents ask their teenagers to give them a tour of their bedrooms. They should ask them questions about their things: "What does this remind you of?" "Why are you glad to own that?" Maybe they could even listen to some of their music! (Remember, the object of this exercise is not for parents to inform teenagers of their opinions regarding their possessions but to learn about their lives!)

After parents have spent some time with their teenagers in their rooms, they should ask (politely) to borrow one object they believe symbolizes a significant prayer request or thanksgiving. They will then spend some time in prayer with this object, thanking God for their teenagers and praying concerning things they've learned about them.

Consider planning a "Parents and Props Prayer Meeting" to which parents can bring "artifacts" from their teenagers' rooms and pray together.

Note to parents: If your teenager isn't too keen on you taking something, *don't*. Make a mental point regarding what prop you would take, and pray with that in mind. Also, don't go into your teenager's room to look for an artifact without his or her permission.

JAVA AND JESUS

Parent meetings don't always have to cover schedules and fund raising. Add some prayer power to your ministry with an early-morning prayer meeting for parents.

Ask parents to join you for a half-hour one weekday morning before work. Before the meeting, prepare index cards with each youth group member's name, and set out some coffee and doughnuts. (After all, what is a church meeting without food?) Bring a few blank index cards for any friends' or siblings' names.

As the parents gather and help themselves to the food, ask for prayer requests and note any specific requests on that youth's index card. Then lead the group in prayer, making sure to pray for each youth group member by name and to include all the prayer requests mentioned. If your group is too large, split into smaller groups and split the cards among the groups. Make sure to end on time so parents won't be late to work.

After the prayer meeting, collect the cards and put them somewhere where they can be kept confidential. You can make this a weekly or monthly event. Next time you can check in with the parents about the requests on the cards and add any new ones.

I'LL PRAY FOR YOURS IF YOU PRAY FOR MINE!

As well as aiming to build better relationships between yourself and parents, encourage parents to get to know and support each other. That way you'll build a stronger foundation for your youth work.

Give each parent a photo of a young person in your group—not his or her own son or daughter—along with the name of the person. Ask the parent to pray for this young person, his or her involvement in the youth work, and his or her relationship with God. Tell the group that you are going to do this, and if anyone doesn't want to be part of it, respect that and don't give out his or her photo.

Don't let anyone know who is praying for whom. After all, it doesn't matter who is praying, just whom we pray to! With that in mind, encourage parents to keep the photos in their Bibles or somewhere private where they'll remember to pray for the young people but where the photos aren't on display to the rest of their families. Somehow praying for someone else's child will mean parents take this more seriously and remember to do it. They'll also be grateful that other people are praying for their sons and daughters and will feel more connected to the other parents in the group.

BUDDING FRIENDSHIPS

One way to help squeeze out criticism and negative attitudes parents may have about the youth program is to involve them in a secret buddy program. Remembering teenagers in the youth group on special days with notes or gifts, acknowledging them for achievements, and encouraging them when they are down will make everyone feel better.

Recruit volunteers who wish to be included, and then draw names. Consider giving teenagers the names of adults to encourage as well!

Positive actions such as generosity and encouragement will squeeze out negativity. By focusing on children other than their own and witnessing how others are encouraging their own sons and daughters, parents will be blessed.

PARENT PRAYER POWER

OK, so some parents would rather walk into a rattlesnake pit than into a room full of teenagers. Dropping off teenagers in the parking lot—no problem. But actually entering the youth room? No, thanks!

Fine. Put those parents to work somewhere else: They can be prayer warriors for your ministry. But rather than ask for prayer in a general, maybe-they-will-maybe-they-won't way, ask parents specifically to pray during your youth meetings.

Recruit a few parents to gather in a classroom elsewhere in the church building during your regularly scheduled youth meetings. While they're there, ask parents to pray for the meeting, the teenagers, and you. There's remarkable power in prayer lifted on behalf of your youth program, *especially* when the people praying are parents.

Don't demand that parents pray in any particular fashion or for any prescribed length of time. Instead, simply ask that they talk with God about blessing and using all that happens in the youth meeting and in the lives of everyone present. If you have detailed prayer requests, share those with your parental prayer warriors.

A key: Do *not* tell teenagers their parents are praying. Instead, let that information emerge naturally as parents ask their kids how a meeting went, or how a prayer was answered. It's life-changing when teenagers discover their parents are praying for them. And it's equally life-changing when the power of parents' prayer is felt in your ministry.

THE GOD FILTER

Choosing a college or university involves many factors, such as expenses, academic programs, and location. Encourage parents to pray for their teenagers' choices and help them add a "God filter" to the decision-making process by asking the following questions:

- Does the academic program you're considering support God's purpose for you?
- Does the school you're considering have good support for your faith, with programs and organizations to help your spiritual growth?
- Is the location of the school near a church you'd be interested in attending?
- Will the program allow you to have a good balance of spiritual and academic life?
- Will this university offer a supportive environment for you to share and defend your worldview?

(Adapted from Group Magazine, January/February 2003)

COVERED WITH PRAYER

Here's a warm way to celebrate your seniors' graduation and send them off blanketed in prayer. Ask parent volunteers to each make a fleece blanket for a high school graduate (not their own children). Ask the parents to commit to praying for their graduates—while they're making the blankets and for at least one full year following graduation. Have parents present the blankets and prayer promises at an event celebrating the seniors.

(Adapted from Group Magazine, March/April 2004)

DOUBLE GAP

The acronym G.A.P. forms the basis for a simple but effective way to structure a program for parents of youth group members.

Gather And Pray: Once a month, during the time the youth group meets, have parents gather at one home to pray for the youth ministry, the teenagers, all the parents, and all the leaders who are working with the kids.

Gather As Parents: Once a quarter, invite parents to meet to discuss issues related to youth ministry activities, culture, and parenting. To encourage discussion, provide parents with copies of youthculture@today from the Center for Parent/Youth Understanding (www.cpyu.org). As alternative discussion starters, copy the Trends section of Group Magazine or download The Home Page, Group Magazine's newsletter for parents. Just go to www.groupmag. com and click on The Home Page.

(Adapted from Group Magazine, July/August 2003)

HEART-TO-HEART

Designating the week of Valentine's Day as Teen Appreciation Week offers a perfect opportunity for affirming teenagers and expanding their horizons beyond the romantic landscape of the holiday.

Recruit parents to each adopt one youth group member for the week before Valentine's Day. During the week, have parents send their adopted teenagers notes of affirmation, special treats, or snacks. End the week with a Teen Appreciation Banquet, a semiformal event that honors the teenagers, either at church or at a restaurant. Have each parent give his or her teenager a small gift, symbolizing God's love for that particular young person.

(Adapted from Group Magazine, January/February 2003)

CONCERTED EFFORT

Strengthen the impact of "prayer partners"—people who are committed to praying daily for specific teenagers—by bringing these adults together for seasonal concerts of prayer.

Enlist an adult volunteer to coordinate the year's program and to recruit those who'll lead each concert section, following the ACTS format of prayer (Adoration, Contrition, Thanksgiving, and Supplication). Pray for specific needs, and besides praying for your church's young people, pray for all those teenagers in your city and in your schools. Also pray for the needs of the season:

- Beginning of a new school year—Many teenagers see this as the *real* beginning of the year. Pray for teenagers as they get a fresh start in a new school year. Pray for their relationships with friends and teachers.
- Christmas holidays—Pray that teenagers will remember the true meaning of the Christmas season, despite all the pressures from non-Christian peers and holiday commercials.
- Approach of prom—This is a stressful time for teenagers. Will they be asked to the prom or not? What will they wear? Will they be able to avoid temptations associated with the event? Pray for teenagers in all these areas.
- Summer break—Some teenagers may be getting jobs during this break, while some may laze away the days of summer. Pray that teenagers will find constructive ways to spend their summer time off. Pray that they will use some of this time to get to know Jesus better.

If your program is based on a year's commitment, schedule a celebratory get-together at the end of the cycle. Not only will your young people benefit from this year of prayer, but also the adults will experience a deepening awareness of prayer, relationship, and involvement.

(Adapted from Group Magazine, September/October 2002)

I GET IT!
BY JOEL FAY

Jeff and Marcie, husband and wife, were enthusiastic volunteers at a Group workcamp. To make it a quality family time, they brought their teenage daughter, Jen. Unfortunately, Jen wasn't very excited about the upcoming week and expected little. *She didn't want to be there.*

Each day passed, and the family was caught up in their duties—serving others by day and experiencing Christian programs at night. One night, after a time of worship, Jen came running up and exclaimed, "I finally get it! All these years you've been dragging me to church, and I finally understand what it's all about!" At that moment she opened her heart to her parents, explaining what she'd experienced during the week and how she had found a new vibrant faith in God. There wasn't a prouder set of parents or a dry eye in the group.

Each year we hear story after story about great "Ah-ha!" moments like this—where something just clicks and kids "get it," where kids discover life lessons and, best of all, a newfound relationship with Jesus.

Mission trips stretch comfort zones, providing an excellent window into the world outside of our own little bubbles. They allow us to get a different perspective and re-evaluate our lives as we experience a new environment, seeing how other people live, what they value, and very often how good we have it at home. A mission trip can soften our hearts and open our minds in remarkable ways.

As a Christian parent, it's heartwarming to see the positive effect on kids that comes from serving others through missions work. Joy. Confidence. Love! We get away from all the distractions of our everyday lives and immerse ourselves in direct service to someone else. And working alongside your son or daughter to help someone else can be an incredible experience. It can "break down walls" so you and your teenager can see each other as real human beings. It can create a neutral environment in which all people, regardless of age or relationship, can share their faith or openly express what's on their heart. What parent wouldn't want some insight into his or her teenager's head or heart?

Surprisingly, though, one of the struggles we hear from youth workers is that they can't get parental involvement. It's as if parents don't feel a mission experience is worth the time and effort. Dave Hoffman, a staff member at Group Publishing, thought he'd have to "burn a week of vacation" the first time he was approached about serving at a Group workcamp. Eventually, he reluctantly "gave up" half a week of vacation to go on a short camp with his son. And Dave "got it." He shared an experience with his son they still talk about today, years later. The very next year he took two weeks of vacation to do missions work and has continued service ever since.

And now it has become a family tradition involving both his son and his daughter, who is now old enough to participate.

Parents like Dave, Jeff and Marcie, and countless others are making a powerful statement that serving others is not something you just talk about in Sunday school. It's something you do. They've shown their children through sweat, hard work, and trust in God that service is a way of life. And in the process, they grow closer as families.

Urge the parents of your students to establish a pattern of service with their kids. It's a chance to make them more aware of the needs of others and to set an example of serving people in need. And if nothing else, the parents might just experience positive and unforgettable moments with their teenagers. Now what parent wouldn't want that?

And in the end, whatever role your parents take—fund-raiser, group leader, chaperone, or volunteer—you're all working together so that even one kid can say, "Hey, I get it!"

Joel Fay was a staff member at the first Group workcamp in 1977 in response to the Thompson Valley flood that killed more than 140 people. Since then, he's lost count of the number of camps he's served at and attended. Joel leads the team that coordinates camps for over 20,000 summer campers domestically and internationally. He has directed large-scale events, taught thousands in workshops, and served as vice president of Group's Camp Services, Sales and Marketing, and Product divisions. He serves his church as elder and chairman of the church board.

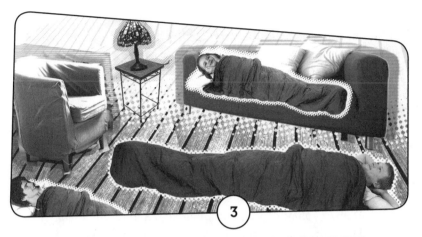

3

BUILDING RELATIONSHIPS
AT HOME

FAMILY FUND-RAISER

Nothing bonds a family like working together to help others. Encourage your students' families to build relationships through a service-oriented fund-raiser.

Challenge families to hold garage sales and then give the proceeds away to organizations that help people in need. To help people get started, hold a planning meeting for all interested families. Then lay out a plan they can follow to do this fund-raiser. Or better yet, find someone in your church who is an experienced "garage saler," and let him or her make a presentation on the best and most efficient techniques to use.

Encourage each family to assign tasks to family members so everyone will have a meaningful way to participate. For example, they can assign tasks such as finding items to sell, pricing the items, setting up displays, advertising, answering customers' questions, and collecting money.

Encourage families to find as much as they can to sell and to think about how they'll be helping someone else by selling their items. If some families don't have enough items to warrant a sale, let them join forces with other families.

You might also give families ideas for places to donate the money they earn.

$20 DREAM DATE

Many families (and especially parents) feel a financial pinch when it comes to the fun-and-recreation part of the budget. But having fun as a family is important for building the strong and healthy relationships that get people through tough times.

One way to increase memory makers for your parents and students is to hold a contest to find the "Ultimate $20 Dream Date." Prepare a set of rules and guidelines for each family, and send them home to the parents and students.

The contest works like this: Each family comes up with the greatest possible idea for a family date that would cost $20 or less, no matter how large the family. Have each family write a description of its idea and turn it in to a youth leader by a designated time.

Once you receive all the ideas, select a winning entry. Then compile all the ideas. At a large family or church function, announce the winner of the contest and treat the whole family to the dream date with a $20 bill.

Spread the other great ideas to your entire ministry. To do this, you can make copies for all the families, include an idea in every student newsletter, put them on your Web site, or send a monthly idea by e-mail. Encourage families to follow through on these relationship-building ideas!

FAMILY FILMMAKING

This fun relationship-building activity is a great way to involve all kinds of skills and personalities in one creative project.

Before this project, find out if you can borrow some video cameras from people in your church (aside from the families represented in your group). It may help if they know the cameras won't be operated by teenagers at some kind of crazy youth event. Collect as many cameras as you can, and bring them to the introductory meeting.

Introduce this project at a youth or parents meeting. Tell families they'll be charged with writing, directing, and producing their own movies to share with each other. They'll have to follow two rules: The finished movies must be appropriate family fare, and each family must involve every member in making the movie.

Give families some time to assign their members special roles, including planning, writing, casting, directing, acting, editing, designing props, catering, and anything else they can think of. Then allow them to use any additional meeting time to begin brainstorming their movies.

At this meeting, find out how many families own video cameras they can use. For families who don't have access to cameras, distribute the cameras you've been able to borrow, and encourage them to share if need be.

Give families a month or so to complete their movies. Then schedule a preview event so everyone can get together and watch the movies families created. You might even want to invite the whole church!

PIZZA PRAYER RECIPE

Most pizza is the result of a phone call and a delivery tip. But *great* pizza is the result of a family cook in the home kitchen. Here is a way to bring youth and their parents together in the kitchen. With the right ingredients, this collaboration can result in great pizza and great relationships. Along with the food ingredients, the right mix of meaningful discussion and thoughtful prayer is the perfect recipe for family success.

To cook up this idea, parents and their youth will set aside one night per week to enjoy pizza, discussion, and prayer. Here is the process for making it happen:
- Find a good pizza recipe.
- Agree on cooking responsibilities.
- Have each family member add a creative ingredient that is representative of his or her experiences during the week.
- While assembling the pizza, discuss each person's choice of a special ingredient.
- While the pizza is cooking, pray for each other and relate to the experiences of each person.
- Enjoy the pizza, and celebrate the opportunity to be together.
Bon appétit!

SPIRITUAL INITIATION

Though often initiation of the spiritual aspect of parent/youth relationships is left to the parent (especially if the teenager is from a Christian home), you can encourage your students to initiate spiritual practices with their parents. This will encourage Christian parents and perhaps challenge or demonstrate caring for non-Christian parents. Challenge youth to converse with their parents regarding spiritual matters, and watch how their parent/child relationships change and grow!

Some specific ideas for initiation include…
- Inviting a parent out for breakfast or ice cream. Encourage students to think about (or write down) a few thoughts or questions they may want to discuss with their parents.
- Initiating spontaneous prayer with the parents, especially when a student and/or parent is worried or concerned about something.

- Planning a family prayer time. This could be before bedtime in the living room or a longer prayer time after a meal.
- Offering to help the parent with a chore (such as doing the dishes) and using that time as an opportunity to talk about God's work in their lives and the world.

REMODELING THE NEST...ONE LAST TIME

With the popularity of home design shows, teenagers may be interested in redesigning their bedrooms! Perhaps the days of middle school pink and purple are over, and they're ready for some leopard print, beads, and art posters. Following is a plan for parents to connect with their teenagers while creating a new atmosphere for their teenagers.

First, have parents determine their family budgets for this venture. Ask parents not to go into debt or dig into the college or vacation fund for this project! Rather, have families work creatively within their means. Parents may want to ask their teenagers if they are willing to chip in. (If a teenager really wants that black light, he or she will probably be willing to help out!)

Second, tell parents to sit down with their teenagers and go over the budget and remodeling design. If a family budget is $75 and the teenager wants a tiled floor, they'll have to do some creative thinking! Remind parents that there are many things they can do very cheaply—rearrange the furniture, clean out clutter, paint walls and/or furniture, buy weird things at the thrift shop, or make a border of old license plates. Knocking out walls, buying new carpet and furniture, and tiling the floor all require big bucks. Remind parents to be realistic! This can be a learning experience about budget and expenses for their teenagers as well as a home design project!

Third, encourage parents and their teenagers to sketch a plan. It doesn't have to be to scale (though that would help), but this will give them a good idea of what they want. If a parent doesn't have a plan, but the teenager knows something needs to be changed, suggest they browse through magazines and watch home design shows. They'll have ideas in no time!

Finally, have families set aside a block of time (a long weekend, perhaps, or two regular weekends in a row) to start working. They should determine who will do what. Have parents teach their teenagers how to paint, pull up carpet, and organize years of clutter! Remember, this is an opportunity for families to work together, so the parents should not allow themselves to get "stuck" doing all the work!

Suggest that families check the Internet for remodeling ideas and techniques or check out the Reader's Digest *New Complete Do-It-Yourself Manual*.

FAMILIES WHO READ TOGETHER...

Creating common ground is key to helping families connect. Suggest a family book discussion to really give parents and teenagers something to talk about.

For the first group, select a book for your teenagers to read together with their parents and other siblings. (Make sure to read the book yourself first and screen it for questionable material.) It could be a Christian book such as Lee Strobel's *The Case for Christ,* Brennan Manning's *The Ragamuffin Gospel,* or something by C.S. Lewis, or a classic or contemporary novel. Try to pick something that will have some relevance to every family member (in other words, don't pick a book that seems to be primarily aimed at males or at females or at, say, motorcycle enthusiasts). If an entire book seems too long to some families, suggest they discuss a chapter or two each time instead.

Have each family set aside some time Sunday afternoons to discuss the book together. You can prepare in advance a list of questions to discuss. You can often find sample questions on the Internet, and many books, novels in particular, come with discussion questions in the back. Encourage families to keep up the tradition on their own. Each month a different family member can pick the book until everyone has had a turn.

BREAKING THROUGH

Each of us can point to particular times in our lives when God has "broken through" our everyday routine, when he has touched our lives in a noticeable way. They may be times of great crisis, when God pointed out a sin in our lives or comforted us in a time of need. Or they could be times of great blessing, when God gave us a tangible gift or created reconciliation in a place where there was none. Have parents try this exercise at home to get them and their teenagers to share some of these moments with each other.

Hand out paper and pens or pencils to each person. You can use colored pencils or markers if you want. Create timelines of your lives, marking important milestones with pictures or notations. You can keep the charts simple, or you can take a great deal of time and make them quite elaborate.

Then talk about the concept of breaking through. Give an example of a "breakthrough" in your own life. Have your family think about this for several minutes, and mark the points on the chart where God has broken through in your lives. Remembering these moments may provoke emotion in some. Ask family members to share some of these moments with each other. Allow several minutes for this. When everyone has finished, close in prayer, thanking God for his persistence in seeking us even when we don't wish to be found.

FAMILY SLEEPOVER

Suggest that families have sleepovers in their living rooms one night. Each family member should bring a sleeping bag or covers and make up a bed on cushions, the sofa, a camp bed, or an air bed. To avoid embarrassment to teenagers, Mom and Dad should sleep in separate beds for this one night!

Families could choose a movie to watch together from the comfort of their beds and get their favorite snacks to eat while they are watching. After lights out, suggest that they share stories of camps they've been to or sleepovers they've had with friends. Can family members remember the first night they spent away from home? Where did they go, and why? How did they feel? Parents may well find that teenagers will open up as they talk in the dark. Families could use this time to talk about other activities they could do together as a family, letting each member choose one thing.

GET COOKING!

Have families cook a meal together—one parent with one teenager. You could simply let the chefs choose the menu or give them a bit more of a challenge. For example, they could ask the other family members to each name their favorite food—the challenge is to incorporate all those foods into one delicious meal. Or they could choose a letter of the alphabet and try to include as many different ingredients beginning with that letter as possible. Parents should let their teenagers play an equal part in planning the meal and cooking it. Parents will need to deliberately stand back and not take over. They don't have to do anything elaborate or fancy; it just needs to be edible! This activity is as much about the process of working together as it is about the result, so don't let anyone off with the excuse that they can't cook! Tell families to decide in advance who will do the washing up—the chefs or the guests—to save arguments on that day. Have families repeat this activity one month later with a different parent and teenager combination being chefs for the evening.

BON APPÉTIT!

To encourage parents and teenagers to spend time together at home, challenge them with this kitchen activity: Cook a special family recipe together.

For added spice, add a secret, unexpected ingredient to the brew, and see how it turns out. Do the other family members notice the change?

This bonding activity could be used to discuss the ingredients that make a family stronger—things like acceptance, service, and communication in healthy measure! What ingredients might spoil the balance? Criticism, indulgence, and selfishness are possibilities.

Debrief with teenagers after their encounter. Give them a chance to share with their classmates about their family meal and even exchange recipes!

SECRET SCRAPBOOKERS

Fans of the scrapbooking craze know that creative page layouts can enhance memories. They also know that building those pages can take a lot of time! Here's how to increase the fun and lessen the work by involving the whole family in a scrapbooking event!

A week or two before the activity, tell youth and their parents to save photos, ticket stubs, brochures, or other memorabilia, and have family members bring their items to the event so they can each create a scrapbook page. You may want to suggest that parents give each family member a few dollars to buy scrapbooking accessories to inspire their creativity.

Have family members draw names to decide which member they will create a page for. When a family member has a birthday, his or her secret scrapbooker presents the designed scrapbook page as a birthday gift. Be sure the secret scrapbooker signs the page with a birthday greeting. After everyone in the family has had a birthday, parents should collect all the pages in an album.

This activity could be done every year so that it becomes a tradition to add to the scrapbook.

(Adapted from Group Magazine, May/June 2003)

FAMILY EASTER RITUALS

Easter is a special time for families to come together. Have families try these ideas to spark teenagers' interest and create Easter memories:

• Spend the Easter afternoon planting flower seeds in small pots to add to a butterfly garden. As you plant the seeds, take turns telling the Easter story and comparing Jesus' resurrection to a butterfly's life cycle.

• Use your teenager's favorite contemporary Christian music for karaoke as a special kind of Easter worship.

• Go for an Easter Sunday ride in the country, and let the youngest driver in your family take the wheel.

• Use a camcorder to videotape your family reading the Easter story and telling what Jesus' resurrection means to each of them. Then save the videotape and compare your answers every year.

(Adapted from Group Magazine, March/April 2003)

NEW YEAR'S TRADITION!

Rituals and traditions are significant threads in the family fabric. And what better time to start a new family tradition than New Year's? Have parents use this idea with their families as a fun way to inspire resolutions based on their family members' unique gifts.

Find a small item for each family member that might encourage that person's talents, such as paints, a harmonica, a journal, or a book. Tie each present to a different color skein of yarn, then hide the gifts somewhere in your house. On New Year's Eve, after everyone goes to bed, weave each yarn throughout the house—around chairs, under couches, in and out of banisters—and tie the end of the yarn to the appropriate family member's doorknob. Along the strings of yarn, tie notes with encouraging Scripture verses or famous quotes.

Then, on New Year's morning, each person must follow his or her string to find the treasure at the end. During breakfast, discuss how these gifts might inspire New Year's resolutions. Continue this tradition each year, offering new opportunities for your family to learn, grow, and rediscover talents.

(Adapted from Group Magazine, November/December 2002)

FAMILY GALLERY

Displaying a family's artwork or creations collectively can bring the family's talents together. Have parents take note of how family members like to express themselves, and encourage them to set aside an area in their home to display everyone's work. Parents can use these suggestions to make their art galleries fun and inspiring:

- Leave out paints, paper, pens, a CD player, an easel, a Bible, and other supplies so inspiration and materials are always available.
- Set up your art gallery in a basement or garage area where your family can paint or draw on the walls of the room. Be sure your kids know the rules about the type of art that's allowed.
- Hold an art show for family members, and discuss interpretations of each other's work. Discuss how art expresses our spirituality.
- Plan a family time of creating artwork together. Make a "collage" that includes all mediums—video or music, painting, writing, and sculpture. Center your collage on a central theme, and encourage every family member to make a contribution.

(Adapted from Group Magazine, September/October 2002)

BUMPER STICKER WISDOM

Stuck to the rear of every other car are statements that alternately amuse, entertain, provoke, and madden. But are they true? Encourage families to use these public "belief statements" to help youth discern whether worldly wisdom holds up under the light of God's Word.

Read each proverb or slogan below, then answer these questions together: How is the statement true? How is the statement untrue? Next, read the Scripture passages and answer the questions that accompany each slogan.

- "Wonder is the beginning of wisdom."—Greek proverb

Read aloud Psalm 111:10; Proverbs 2:6; and James 1:5-6; 3:13-18. Ask: How true is this statement when weighed against Scripture? What did you learn about wisdom from these verses?

- "Talking is easy; action is difficult." —Spanish proverb

Read aloud Luke 6:46-49 and James 1:19-25; 2:14-26. Ask: What do these verses have to say about listening? speaking? doing? How are actions tied to faith? How easy or difficult is it for Christians to "walk their talk"?

- "Visualize world peace."—bumper sticker

Read John 14:27; Romans 5:1-2; Ephesians 2:11-18; and Hebrews 12:14. Ask: What kind of peace is this bumper sticker referring to? How is peace defined in these passages? How is the peace the Bible talks about different from or similar to the peace that's conveyed in the slogan?

Family Fun: Go to a large parking lot together and search for interesting bumper stickers. Write them down, then go home and discuss them using the strategy above.

(Adapted from Group Magazine, May/June 2000)

FIVE REASONS I LOVE MY TEENAGERS…AND MY DREAM FOR THEIR SPIRITUAL GROWTH
BY JENNY BAKER

It's an interesting question to have to answer: Why do I love my teenagers? My immediate reaction is "because I just do," but for this book, I needed to go a little deeper than that. And this is where my thinking has led me…

Because they are a gift from God.

My sister's first daughter lived for only nine hours. My sister-in-law found it difficult to conceive and has just one very precious son. One of my best friends is exploring fertility treatment because she and her husband would love to have children but so far haven't been able to. So I am very aware that my two boys are a gift from God. I don't deserve them; I have no right to have them. They have been entrusted to me and Jonny, my husband, to love and to bring up, with help from family and friends. I don't want to take that for granted, and I'm grateful to God for giving me the privilege of being an important part of their lives.

Because they are not like me.

Well, they are a bit like me. Joel has dark curly hair and brown eyes like me. Harry has the same pedantic attention to detail that I do. But they are their own unique selves, and that's something I've come to appreciate the hard way. I was a very miserable, shy, lonely teenager, always longing for a good friend and wanting to belong to a group.

One of my boys is very happy in his own company and doesn't seem to need a big gang of friends around him. But instead of recognizing that straightaway, I immediately started to project my own teenage issues onto him. I thought that he was lonely and shy, like I used to be; I worried that he didn't have any good friends and was unhappy, like I used to be. I felt that I needed to interfere and rescue him from the despair that I used to feel. My wise husband helped me see that our boy is fine—he has lots of friends at school; he's happy and easygoing; he's just himself. And I need to realize that and let him be. He'll find his own angst; I don't need to give him mine.

Because they are different from each other.

I first noticed this in the way each of my young sons ate a sandwich. Joel used to carefully eat around the crust and save the soft bread and filling until the end. Harry would dive in and eat the center and then try to leave the crusts. You can probably see it with your own children—that even though they've been brought up in the same family, in the same house, with the same parents, they have different tastes, different gifts, different personalities, and different needs. The trick for us is to try to respect those differences and allow them to flourish. Treating them fairly does not necessarily mean treating them identically, and that's an important thing for them to learn.

Because they are fun, creative, and nice to be with.

I don't want this to sound smug, and I'm aware that things may change in the future, but I think my two boys are both really wonderful people. I know I'm biased because I'm their mom, and I'm not suggesting for a minute that they are perfect, and I hope I would still love them even if they fought all the time and were horrible. Have I given enough qualifiers?! The reason I've included this one is that we hear so much about how terrible teenagers can be—rude, self-centered, disrespectful, and rebellious—that we almost expect them to fill that stereotype and can start to relate to them as if they did. But treat them with dignity and high expectations as reasonable, fun, capable people, and they'll rise to the challenge.

Because it's my job to.

When their bedrooms are complete dumps again and the newly ironed shirts that I have just given them for school next week end up crumpled on the floor, I'm their mom. When they sulk or answer back or get angry over some small thing, I'm their mom. When they argue over who is going to sit in the chair opposite the TV for the 900th time, I'm their mom. When they moan because they have to do the dishes or are late arriving home without letting me know where they were, I'm still their mom. It's my job to love my boys, to be their biggest fan, to fight for them if I need to, and to help them become men of God—and I want to do that to the best of my ability.

As my boys grow in their relationships with God, I hope and pray that they find good Christian friends to journey with, as I know how important that has been to me—people who love God and want to walk in his ways; people who will talk theology with them and help them work things out in their own minds; people who will stand by them when things are difficult and whom they can help in turn; people who will challenge them, love them, and value them.

I hope Joel and Harry will each get to a place where they really need God and are totally dependent on God so they can learn from experience that his love for them is fierce and his knowledge of them is complete. And I know that that may be difficult for me to see—I'll need to stand back and not interfere; I'll need to let them find their own way; I'll need to resist the temptation to rescue and let God do that instead.

I pray that my boys will grow up with a broad, holistic view of the kingdom of God, to understand that God is passionate about redeeming every part of his good creation and that he wants them to get involved in that. I hope that Micah 6:8 will describe the way that they choose to live: "To act justly and to love mercy and to walk humbly with your God."

And if none of that happens, I'll still be their mom, and I'll still love them!

Jenny Baker has been dedicated to innovative youth ministry for nearly 16 years. She worked for Youth for Christ for a decade and now writes for several Christian organizations, including the United Kingdom's Youthwork magazine. She is a member of Grace, the alternative worship community in west London. Jenny is a trustee of Greenbelt, the U.K. Christian arts festival, and is the author of Transforming Prayers, *published by Group.*

THIS MONTH'S
YOUTH
MINISTRY
EVENTS:

• MON. THE 14TH
BAKE SALE

• THUR. THE 17TH
FIELD TRIP

• SUN. THE 20TH
CONCERT

• TUE. THE 29TH
BOOK CLUB

4

KEEPING PARENTS INFORMED

10-TO-1

So you believe in the importance of keeping parents informed about what's happening in youth ministry. But does that mean you have to do it all yourself? No way! Assign your volunteer staff to do this job in bite-size chunks.

Compile a list of all the parents of your group members. Assign 10 of those parents to each of your volunteer staff members. Or if you're lucky enough to have more than enough volunteers for this job, assign people fewer than 10 parents.

If you don't have enough volunteers to cover all the parents, consider recruiting some parents or other volunteers specifically to serve in this capacity—just to pass information along to groups of 10 parents.

Charge your volunteers with the task of contacting their assigned parents once a month to tell them what events are coming up and what the group needs (resources, volunteer help, drivers, and so on).

While they're at it, this would be a great opportunity for volunteers to tell parents specifically what the group enjoys about their kids. This is a great way to make sure parents look forward to these phone calls!

PARENT PLACARD

If you have a fun-loving congregation, use this wacky idea to get parents' attention.

Use two pieces of cardboard or poster board to create a placard—you know, those advertising signs people wear like a sandwich to call attention to products or services (or to remind people that the end of the world is near).

Decorate your two signs with information about youth ministry events coming up for the next month. Then tie the pieces of cardboard or poster board together at the tops and on the sides so an adult will be able to wear the placard around.

Then find a fun-loving and confident parent who doesn't mind attracting a little attention (any politicians in your church?). Tell that parent it is his or her turn to wear the placard at church each week for a month. Give that person a bell as well. It will help attract attention.

The parent wearing the placard should walk around ringing the bell, finding other parents, and informing them of what's going on in the youth ministry during the next month.

The parent who wears the placard gets to choose the next month's lucky parent. (You'll need to make new signs every month, with that month's information.)

For extra fun, consider giving the placard parent a bullhorn so he or she can obnoxiously make announcements as well.

BE A TEASE

With the advent of voice mail, e-mail, and instant messaging, good ol' regular mail has declined in use and popularity. However, a well-timed regular "snail mail" message will not only inform parents and youth of coming events but also create enthusiasm for the event.

Postcards are a great and inexpensive way to both communicate information and create this enthusiasm, especially if the postcards are creatively done. Teaser postcards are especially effective. These are sent out prior to an event even being announced (or being fully explained) and create a sense of curiosity, mystery, and anticipation. Postcards can also help you get the date marked on family calendars. Since the postcards are meant to have only a small amount of teaser information, be sure the church's return address is on them so families know the information is regarding a church event. Here are some teaser ideas:

- For any event—It is Saturday, Oct. 13. Do you know where your teenager is?

- For a video scavenger hunt—Can your youth find 10 fire hydrants? Find out at 4:30 p.m. on Oct. 13!
- For an announced retreat where you plan to do a game/activity using a strange item (in this case, candy fish)—At this year's retreat, think FISH. Registration ends Oct. 13.
- For any event—I know the place to be on Oct. 13. Do you?
- For a picnic/food event—We make stomachs happy. October 1.

Each of the above is addressed to the parents but could be tweaked to be sent directly to the youth. For instance, the first one would read, "It is Saturday, October 13. Do you know where *you* are?"

Remember that the goal is to create curiosity and interest as well as to get the date marked on family calendars. So be creative in your postcards, and watch the anticipation for your events grow.

NOT A YOUTH MINISTER

Many of us have had those "watershed" moments, times a simple conversation produces an idea that is ministry-altering. A youth minister friend and I were eating breakfast together and discussing some of the ups and downs of our ministries. As we talked about some of our more troubled youth, we kept finding ourselves referring to the youth's difficult family situation or to the youth's relationship with parents. As we struggled to find ways to care for youth in this context, my friend said to me, "You know, we are not really *youth* ministers. We are *family* ministers."

I stared at him for a minute and quickly began to realize that my whole perspective on youth ministry was about to change. I had never been so naive as to think that I could deal with youth without dealing with their families, but I only believed this in theory. In practice, I dealt almost exclusively with the youth, only dealing with parents in times of crisis or when chaperones were needed. But with that breakfast conversation, I realized that my whole perspective needed to change.

As a result, I started doing some things differently—some things you might want to try as you minister to your youth:
- As kids enter the youth group, meet with them and their families, trying to have a meal not just with the teenager but with Mom, Dad, Sister, and Brother. Get into the teenagers' houses as often as you can, getting a feel for what life is like in their homes.
- Create a newsletter section "Just for Parents" that gives them ideas of what they can do with and for their youth. Youth activities become more parent-friendly as you ask parents to join you for the beginning

or end portions of your youth meetings. Additionally, simply ask more questions of the kids regarding their families, not only to build your own understanding but also to show the youth that you want insight into this large and crucial part of their lives.

Your impact on the students will always be limited if you don't attempt to understand their families. So expand on your understanding of what it means to care for the youth: Begin to see yourself as a *family* minister.

YOU NEVER TOLD ME

Youth workers will always run into the phrases "You never told me" and "I didn't know." But you can do a media blitz that will make those phrases far less likely.

Here are the standard lines of communication. Send out information regarding the "who, what, when, where, and how much" of every event you do through all of these channels:

- Use a snail-mail newsletter with a monthly calendar.
- Compile an e-mail list with all your parents' addresses, and send them a note one week prior to every event.
- Host at least one meeting a year to tell them about what they can expect in the year to come.
- Compile a phone calling tree, staffed with your adult leaders, and have them ready to call all parents for information regarding your biggest events.

Just for fun, once a quarter send students home with an object lesson to parents that invites them into your media connections. For instance, send home a newsletter tucked halfway inside an aluminum can that students have decorated to read, "CAN we talk?" The letter will explain all the ways parents can stay in touch with you.

REFRIGERATED FACTS

Ever have problems getting your youth and their parents to remember upcoming events? This is an awesome way to put the information in their homes on the most-visited appliance in the house. Every visit to the refrigerator will present a reminder of upcoming youth events.

This idea is low tech with highly effective results. Provide teenagers with refrigerator magnet frames. With a little magnetism, listed reminders, and a receptive fridge, your youth and parents will be better informed.

Supply one refrigerator magnet frame per student. The opening of the frame should be about 3x5 inches. On a monthly basis, make a list of activities for that month. Give youth a copy of the list on a 3x5-inch piece of paper. Provide a contact phone number at the bottom of the list so parents or youth can call to get details regarding any of the monthly activities. Since the refrigerator is probably the most valuable appliance in the home, it will be a continual reminder to youth and their parents that youth group is most valuable and awaiting their participation. Refrigerating the facts preserves them for future use!

PRESS CONFERENCE

To inform parents about the happenings in your youth group, invite them to a "press conference" where they are able to ask several youth (preferably ones well-informed about what's happening and why) any questions they wish.

You can make this fun by having the youth dress up in professional clothes—well-ironed suits (pick up some retro ones from the thrift store), ties, and dark-colored shoes. Have other students design some sort of emblem to hang behind the podium. Have a microphone and several "security guards" on the stage.

In case the parents are too surprised to ask questions, plant a few youth around them to ask questions. Some of their questions could be legitimate; others could be ridiculous. Example: "Miss Brown, I heard that they're considering changing the toilet paper from Scott to some fluffy sort with pictures of pink elephants on it. Is that true?" "No, it's not. It will be pictures of hippos in tutus. It's just a rumor about the elephants."

This is a great activity to do if you're afraid parents aren't getting fliers you send home or if there's been some sort of misunderstanding about an event or project.

CYBER-PARENTS

What's the best way of getting your attention? Do you prefer to be called? sent a letter? sent an e-mail? Or do you like things in writing on pristine white paper? Whatever your preference, you can be sure that not everyone is like you. So when it comes to communicating with parents, use a variety of methods so you can be sure to deliver your message in a way that will suit as many people as possible.

One key to communicating with busy, working parents is e-mail. They'll be used to sorting through the messages in their in-boxes and dealing with them, and although their teenagers aren't part of their working lives, for parents who use e-mail every day at work, this is a strategic way to bring your activities to their attention. So get e-mail addresses of parents, and send out news and reminders by e-mail as well as on paper for those who don't have e-mail. Don't send too many—you don't want to be treated like spam!

EYE-TO-EYE CONTACT

When you first read this idea, you may think it's creating more work for you just for the sake of it, but stick with it and you'll see the reasoning behind it! Instead of sending newsletters or program details through the mail or home with kids, get out and deliver them by hand to each teenager's home. Knock on the door, and hand them over to parents—don't put them in the mailbox! This brings you into direct contact with parents, giving you an opportunity to introduce yourself if you haven't met before. They'll appreciate the effort you are putting into getting to know them, and when they see you on the doorstep, they may well invite you in for coffee and a chat. If you can't do this for all your kids every time there's a letter to their parents, then send some through the mail and deliver the others, making sure that you visit each home once a year.

TACKY TIME

To get parents involved and keep them informed about upcoming events, designate a bulletin board or wall in the church that can be used for posting youth group events.

Ask teams of students and parents to take turns updating the board monthly with new pictures and upcoming events.

Give ridiculous prizes for those teams that go all out.

BIG QUESTION NIGHT

You may be familiar with the idea of inviting teenagers to submit their questions for a Q-and-A time, but how about encouraging parents to do the same?

Once or twice a year, hold a Big Question Night. Let parents know one or two weeks ahead of time that you'll be attempting to answer any and all questions they bring. Also let them know that although you probably won't have all the answers on the spot, you'll be willing to do follow-up research.

Invite feedback from the parents as you go along, and you'll generate lively discussion. Take notes so you can expand on popular topics at a later time.

(Adapted from Group Magazine, March/April, 2003)

PARENTS AS ALLIES
BY RICK LAWRENCE

As editor of Group Magazine, I'm always talking with youth leaders, picking their brains and listening to their woes. Not long ago at a convention, I invited six randomly snagged youth workers to lunch so I could ask them what hurdles they faced in their ministries.

After a few get-to-know-you comments, they launched into a topic that burned through the next 45 minutes—uninvolved, spiritually apathetic, morally confused, and hyperbusy *parents*. These six youth workers—from different denominations, locations, and backgrounds—were so angry and frustrated with parents that the atmosphere quickly devolved into a "top this one" contest.

As the fiery arrows flew, I remembered the big survey we'd recently completed with youth leaders from around the world. We asked them to tell us their top complaints about youth ministry, then we categorized their answers. "Lack of parental involvement" whack-a-moled all the other responses, representing the top complaint of more than half (54 percent) of all those we surveyed. Nothing else even came close (although I found it interesting that "the church bus" garnered 3 percent of the votes).

Youth leaders have always had a love-hate relationship with their group members' parents, but in the last few years, I've seen a significant spike in complaints about them. And these aren't just casual complaints; there's a lot of anger fueling them.

Parents, of course, are an easy target for youth leaders—you have a front-row seat to the pain and destruction caused by bad parenting. So many parents use the church as a faith "service provider" that'll fill their kids' faith tank at a bargain price. The worst ones are either incredibly absent from their kids' lives or incredibly abusive.

As I listened to these lunchtime youth ministers vent about the rotten things parents do to screw up their kids, I realized they were doing what any pagan could do—skewer the people who annoy, vex, and anger us.

Finally, a soft-spoken woman who'd remained relatively quiet through it all said, "I've struggled with why parents make the choices they do. They love their kids, but they need help. They need to know how important they are in the faith development process." She went on to describe how she's proactively offered parent training classes, father-son/mother-daughter experiences, and mentoring opportunities to her kids' parents.

Her response quickly silenced the others. That's because her proactive strategy acknowledged the problems but did something to engage them. I think the others felt exposed—deep inside we know that complaining *alone* does nothing. Instead of attacking her "enemies," she approached them in "the opposite spirit."

This youth leader "got it." More than any other factor (by far), parents are responsible for helping their teenagers grow in Christ. In a Group Magazine survey of more than 10,000 Christian kids, one in five (17.9 percent) chose their parents' influence as their number one catalyst for spiritual growth. Another fifth (18.2 percent) said parents were their number two or number three influence. That jibes well with Search Institute's top two "predictors of a mature faith" in teenagers: (1) Kids who often "talk about faith with their mother" and (2) Kids who often "talk about faith with their father" are most likely to stay committed to Christ.

Simply put, parents' spiritual maturity is more important than our own in impacting our group members for Christ. And that means it's vital we invest in parents' spiritual growth and work hard to provide opportunities for them to engage their own kids around issues of faith. If you can get parents to see themselves as the primary catalysts for faith growth in their kids' lives *and then actually do something with their kids as a result,* your ministry will explode.

I think this is the crucial turning-point issue for today's youth ministers. I feel so strongly about it that I helped create the National Network of Youth Ministries' "A Call to Youth Ministers and the Church." Read the "call" and then sign it by going to www.youthworkers.net/parents.

Once you buy into your parents' potential for the deepest impact, you'll be motivated to serve and equip them for ministry to their own kids. There's nothing more crucial on your plate right now.

Rick Lawrence has been editor of Group Magazine for 17 years.

HELPING PARENTS UNDERSTAND THEIR KIDS' WORLD

PARENT FIELD TRIP

Ah, how quickly we forget what it's like to be young. This idea will help remind your students' parents (and you!).

Take a small group of parents on a field trip to a local teenage hangout. Ideally, none of their kids should be there at the time. The group should be small enough that you won't attract a lot of attention, change the way the teenagers act, or drive them away. Kind of like watching lions roam the Serengeti—you want to see them in their natural habitat.

Spend some time observing the students. Pay attention to the way they act, the way they treat each other, what seems to make them feel comfortable and uncomfortable, and what's important to them.

After you observe for a while, take your small group of parents somewhere else—somewhere *they'll* be comfortable. Have a good discussion about what your group saw, what you think it's like to be a teenager, and what their kids experience on a daily basis. Then talk about ways you can work together to support teenagers as they navigate the tricky teenage world.

OTHER PEOPLE'S KIDS

Give parents a way to find out what it's like to be a teenager—without having to ask their own kids. Organize some "other people's kids" nights for parents and teenagers who are interested in understanding each other better.

Assign parents to small groups (three to five parents). Create small groups of teenagers (about the same size) who are comfortable with each other and who like to hang out together. Include both boys and girls in a group whenever possible. Encourage everyone to be open and honest with each other.

Match up small groups of parents with small groups of teenagers. Make sure none of the parents have their own kids in their group. Arm the parents with some suggested questions (see below), and send these groups out for pizza and conversation. After group members have gotten to know each other a bit, parents can ask the kids questions about what it's like to be a teenager. Here are some questions they might want to ask:

- What's your favorite thing to do on a Friday night?
- What are your plans for the future?
- What do you wish your parents knew about teenagers?
- What's the best thing your parents have done for you?
- What do you wish you had more time for?
- What do you like to do with your parents?
- Whom do you admire the most?

Remember, the students might also want to ask questions about what it's like to be a parent!

TEEN MAGAZINES

In trying to help parents understand their kids' world, why not turn to popular media? Between the Internet, MTV, 24-hour news channels, and reality television shows alone, teenagers are bombarded with messages that are relativistic and self-centered at best. But parents and youth workers sometimes overlook another medium teenagers pay a lot of attention to—teenage magazines and fashion magazines. These magazines help dictate what is cool and acceptable in the youth subculture.

Before a parents meeting, collect or purchase teenage and fashion magazines so each pair of parents can share one magazine. Have parents form pairs with people they aren't married to. Give each pair about 15 minutes to look through the magazine and discuss the following issues:

- What is the primary theme of this magazine?
- What are some feelings teenagers would have about themselves while reading through this magazine?

• What are some feelings teenagers would have about the world around them while reading through this magazine? What does it say about peers? parents? school? authority? church? religion?

After 15 minutes, have everyone gather and share his or her thoughts on the three discussion questions.

After each person gets to share, brainstorm ways parents can safely and respectfully engage in conversation with their teenagers about these themes and feelings. Then help parents share ideas for providing their kids with positive messages and building strong, Christlike character.

Close with prayer while focusing on spirit-guided wisdom for these much-needed conversations.

IN OR OUT

As we sat around the youth room, Rachel Stoffer was chatting and laughing with her friends when her dad walked in. Another youth greeted him with a chipper, "Hey, Mr. Stoffer!" To Rachel's wide-eyed horror, Mr. Stoffer replied, "'Sup, Dawg!"

Ouch! For many youth, the pain of watching their parents try to be "in" or "cool" with their friends is almost more than they can bear. However, oftentimes parents have the right idea: They are trying to stay clued in to their kids' lives by being clued in to their kids' culture. Help them do this (without embarrassing themselves or their kids) by creating the following activity for kids to do at home with their parents. The activity could be sent home as part of a parent or youth group newsletter or could be an "assignment" kids do at home after a youth group meeting about relating with their parents.

You will need to create a page (or more) broken into large squares, similar to the one here:

In each square you should type an item, such as "sneakers," "smoking," or "playing pool." Students and parents will cut up the grids and make a stack of the items. Then, taking turns, the students and parents draw cards. The parent is to think about the item or issue on the card in relation to the teenager's age and culture; the youth is to think about the item on the card in relation to when the parent was the same age he or she is. Seeing the item, both the parent and the youth state whether they think that activity or thing would be considered "in," "out," or "neutral" for the other person's culture. Parents and youth then discuss the item and the response given by each.

In addition to the items above, here are some others that you could put in the boxes: roller-skating, playgrounds, V-neck T-shirts, camping, outdoor concerts, beer, football, science fiction, comic books, miniskirts, the beach, road trips, big hair, having a job, sleepovers, boots.

EYE ON CULTURE

Parents often go to extremes when evaluating their kids' culture. Some immediately condemn it with gasps and looks of shock and disdain. Others too readily accept all aspects of the culture, simply expecting that "kids will be kids." Both of these extremes can lead to disaster, and usually neither is based on a well-thought-out view of their kids' world.

To help parents think more deeply and wisely about the world their teenagers are living in, encourage them to do some observation. Have parents go somewhere their youth might be found: the mall, a high school basketball game, or the local mini-golf course on a Friday night. Have them sit for 30 minutes and observe the youth they see. Provide the following set of questions for parents to answer as they observe:

- Describe how the young people you see are dressed. How do you feel about their dress?
- Describe how the young people are acting. Would you say it is typical? Why or why not?
- Describe the different "groups" or "cliques" of youth you have observed.
- Describe what seems to make the kids laugh.
- From your observations only, what seems to be important to the youth?

After the parents do the observation and answer the questions, they should talk with their own kids about what they observed and let the youth see the answers and respond to them. Then the parents and youth should talk about the issues that were raised in the parents' minds. This is a great way to get teenagers and parents talking about important issues without necessarily confronting an issue currently present in their own parent-child relationship.

You may also want to provide this activity prior to a parent meeting and have parents bring their results to the meeting. You could then lead a discussion of their findings and give ideas for responding to their own youth.

FROM PAPERBACKS TO PAPERLESS

If you're going to explain the world of teenagers to parents, a handout won't do. Make parents enter into the world of teenagers a bit and search the Web. Rather than just reading about teenagers, parents can see how teenagers see things.

There are many accessible Web-page-making software programs. If you don't know how, one of your teenagers definitely does. Create a page that lists "The 10 Key Trends for Teenagers." Your list might include "The latest in cell phones," "Data on divorce," "College prep," and "Translating slang." Each trend can link to another page that gives visual images, Web links to further information, and articles from culture watchers.

An alternative approach would be to create a blog or "Web log," an online journal that describes your experiences with teenagers and the changing trends of their culture. To find out how, just do an Internet search for "blog" or "online journal."

TREASURE HUNTING: PARENTAL PIRATING

Ahoy, mate! Here is a fun way for parents to learn about their teenagers. In order to understand youth, parents must understand the world as their teenagers see it. Use this entertaining and bonding activity to give parents and youth a better understanding of each other.

Have the youth create a treasure chest filled with items that are important to them. Their parents will be invited to an intriguing treasure hunt. Parents will follow clues to uncover the hidden location of the treasure chest. In the end, everyone will share in the booty.

Ask teenagers to contribute one or two items each that they believe represent their world. They will place these items along with candy into a box (or boxes if needed). They will wrap the box in plain white paper and use markers to give it the appearance of a treasure chest.

Have invitations for the youth to take home to their parents, inviting parents to a treasure hunt party. Prior to the treasure hunt, hide the treasure chest. Then create a list of clues revealing the location of the treasure.

At the treasure hunt party, divide the parents and youth into teams. Each team will get a list of clues. When the treasure chest is discovered, call everyone together. The youth will explain the meaning of the contents they contributed to the treasure chest. Enable a discussion about youth and their world. With a better understanding of each other, everyone will share in consuming the booty (candy). Happy hunting!

A DAY IN THE LIFE

When this generation's parents were in high school, text messaging, cell phones, and reality TV music stars did not exist! Unless parents hang out with their teenagers day after day for several weeks (even going to school with them), they won't connect with the lives their teenagers are living. (And even if they could hang out with their teenagers all the time, everyone would treat them differently because they're a product of a different generation.)

So recruit the journalists in your youth group, and commence making "A Day in the Life of Me." Find writers, photographers, and videographers. Have students make a documentary of their lives and daily experiences. Give them these questions as a starting point:

- What sorts of people do you see every day?
- Where do some of the issues you struggle with come from?
- What does your "world" expect of you?
- Are you "free"? Why or why not? What sorts of things trap you?
- What is the most important thing for others to know about your world?
- What symbols are significant within your (and your peers') lives?

Once they've had a chance to think about some of these questions, start the project. Determine a time limit (one week, one month, one semester) when the students will be asked to share their documentaries with the parents of the youth group. Perhaps some have worked as a team; perhaps others have worked alone. Figure out a compilation (using bits from each), or if there are fewer documentaries, plan to present them all.

Invite parents to "A Day in the Life of Me," in which students will share their work. Allow for questions at the end. Try to make this a time of sharing lives and stories and not a time to discuss opinions on how some of the problems can be "fixed" or dealt with.

HOW WAS YOUR DAY?

One of the best ways to understand a young person's world is to get him or her to talk about it while you listen, but as most parents know, that can sometimes be very difficult! This conversation will be all too familiar:

Parent: How was your day today?

Teenager: All right.

Parent: What happened?

Teenager: Nothing much.

In a newsletter, give your parents this list of 10 questions to ask teenagers to try to get them to open up:

- What was the coolest (or strangest, or most frustrating) thing that happened at school today?
- (After watching a movie or TV program) Which character do you think was most like you? Why? Or which character would you like to swap places with, and why?
- How would you rate your evening on a scale of 1 to 10? Why's that?
- What's made you laugh recently?
- What was the highlight of your day? What was the low point?
- If you could change one thing about your school (or youth group or even this family!), what would it be? Why's that?
- (About a computer game they're playing) What's going on in this level? What do you have to do to get to the next level?
- What's the most interesting thing you've learned this week at school?
- What age have you most enjoyed being so far in your life? What age would you most like to be? Why's that?
- What's the best thing someone has done for you this week?

Ask parents to let you know which ones worked and to send you their favorite questions. You could include those in the next newsletter.

A GOOD READ

Parents will often suggest books they think their children should read, so how about doing it the other way around? Suggest that parents read what their teenagers have chosen to read and have enjoyed reading—after their teenagers have finished, of course! It doesn't have to be a book—it could be a magazine, a comic, or even a favorite Web site that they like to visit. Encourage parents to reflect on why they think their teenagers enjoyed this material. What is attractive about it? What might they have learned from it? Suggest that parents talk to their teenagers about it and ask questions in order to understand, not to judge. If there's something in the material that parents disagree with, encourage them to get their teenagers to critique that part—to ask questions and explore the characters' actions and motivations. They should aim to help their teenagers see for themselves what's questionable about the material instead of just telling them where it's wrong.

CLIP SERVICE SUPREMO

It's a challenge to keep up with what's hot and what's not in Teen World. Fads come and go with lightning speed, but parents are usually aware of them. After all, when your little girl can't pass through airport security because of her body piercings, it's tough not to notice.

But *trends*—those gradual shifts in culture that sometimes fly under the radar—are tough for parents to track.

So help out.

As you read Group Magazine or Youthworker Journal, take note of articles that address trends in the lives of young people. Make copies of the appropriate articles, and send them to parents along with a quick note explaining how the article is relevant to your youth group or their teenagers.

Don't skip the note. If you send a body-piercing article blind, without any accompanying letter, parents will panic and begin running metal detectors over their kids to ferret out hidden studs.

This occasional clip service not only helps parents understand their kids' world but can also spark great discussions within families.

And it doesn't hurt that parents will be forced to admit that you do more than hang out at the park shooting baskets. You keep up on your professional reading, too!

FASHION FRUGAL

Are your teenagers demanding the latest trendy clothes, such as J.Crew, Tommy Hilfiger, or Abercrombie & Fitch? Fashion is important to teenagers, but many parents cannot afford the latest styles to keep their teenagers looking hip. Here are some ideas you can give parents to help reconcile their kids' needs with their budgetary restraints. (And they might just find that working together on this gives them some family bonding time they've been looking for!)

- Talk about current fashion trends as a family. Ask why particular fashions are important.
- Discuss your family clothing budget. Tell your teenager how much you can afford to spend on clothes.
- Comb the Sunday paper together for good sales.

(Adapted from Group Magazine, September/October 2002)

BUZZWORD

Use a video camera to draw teenagers from your local high schools into discussions on serious topics such as racism, sexuality, social justice, depression, and "Who was Jesus?" Plan to show the video at a parent meeting in order to help parents understand their kids' world.

Set up a table in a high-traffic area frequented by high schoolers—for example, a shopping mall, a park, an outdoor recreation area, or on school grounds (be sure to get necessary permission ahead of time). Then ask teenagers questions connected to the Buzz Topic of the Week. If kids give permission, videotape their answers, and tell them the videos will be played at the next parent meeting. Invite teenagers to attend the meeting at whatever time and place works best for your youth group.

Design the meeting as a guided discussion where people are free to express their opinions, not as a Bible study or lesson. As parents and young people share views in the dialogue, however, they'll be able to express biblical truth to teenagers who'd never come to a Bible study, and parents will gain valuable insights into their teenagers' lives.

(Adapted from Group Magazine, September/October 2002)

EQUIPPING PARENTS TO KNOW YOUTH CULTURE
BY WALT MUELLER

I'm a pretty average-looking 48-year-old man. That might be why I get so many funny looks when I go to the mall. The cashiers think I'm either a crazed middle-aged maniac or a terrible father. On one recent mall excursion, I stood in line at the bookstore to purchase a stack of magazines including YM, Seventeen, Thrasher, Rolling Stone, and Tattoo Savage. Then I went next door to the music store to pick up the latest albums by Usher, Dave Matthews, and Avril Lavigne. When I catch people glancing curiously back and forth between me and my armload of goodies, I quickly utter what I'm sure comes off sounding like a pretty lame excuse: "I study youth culture for a living." I can always tell what they're thinking: "Yeah, right."

If you're serious about reaching today's emerging generation with the gospel, you've probably stood in the same line and gotten the same stares. The reason? You know that the culture of your students is rapidly changing. You know it's a culture different from your own. And you know that this reality makes God's call to "go into their world" a call to cross-cultural missions. Your mall trips—like mine—are a necessary part of your cross-cultural ministry preparation. But do you realize that when it comes to doing cross-cultural ministry in their world, you are only a "secondary" missionary? That's right. God has made it clear that parents are the people he's called to be primarily responsible for the spiritual nurture of their children. Your role is to come alongside these "primary" missionaries and assist them as they fulfill their God-given role. As someone who spends significant time with students, you have unique access to them and their world. So what, if anything, are you doing to help parents connect with their kids by helping them understand and connect with kids' culture?

Here are some simple steps you can take to help parents become more "youth-culture literate" and effective in their role of nurturing their children in the faith as they grow up in the midst of a powerful and pervasive youth culture.

First, let parents know you are going to shoot straight with them about youth culture…and they'll love you for it! Early on in my youth ministry, I erroneously believed that I had nothing at all to say to parents. After all, I wasn't a parent myself. Pretty soon, my faulty thinking was challenged as a group of parents came to me to ask for "help."

"But I'm not a parent," I said. "I can't tell you how to parent your kids."

They told me, "That's not what we want. You spend time with them, and you know their world. Tell us as much as you can about their world."

I began to look for ways to share the reality of youth culture with them on a regular basis. They didn't like what they heard. It was new, strange, and sometimes frightening. But they loved me for opening their eyes to the pressures, challenges, problems, choices, and expectations facing their teenagers. Without that knowledge of the real issues, they couldn't consciously respond with Christlike wisdom and advice.

Second, encourage parents to use the youth culture knowledge you're sharing with them in prophetic, preventive, and redemptive ways. Their prophetic role is to proclaim God's truth regarding the issues their teenagers are sure to face. For example, knowing the facts about teenagers' sexual values and behaviors will spur them on to apply God's Word to those specific values and behaviors with their own kids.

In their preventive role, parents can take what they know and prepare their children to avoid participation in behaviors that are sinful and wrong, while encouraging them to enjoy those aspects of youth culture that are positive. When it comes to sexuality, help parents develop strategies for pointing their kids into making good and Christlike choices.

Then prepare them to fulfill their redemptive role by pointing them to helpful resources they can use when they have to intervene in crisis. For example, if substance abuse becomes an issue for a student, prior knowledge of how to respond and where to refer will be greatly appreciated by struggling parents. The redemptive role is important yet oftentimes overlooked. Don't buy the lie that "it can't happen in our church families." The reality is that it probably already does.

Third, pass on everything you learn about youth culture, and point parents to resources that will help them go further. In many ways, you're called to function as an advance scout. You need to have your ear to the ground in order to know what's coming over the youth-culture horizon long before it gets here. Let parents know what you're hearing by passing on quotes, statistics, research findings, lyrics, and other information you "discover" in your day-to-day ministry and observation. In addition, point them to helpful youth-culture Web sites that are updated regularly, including the Center for Parent/Youth Understanding (www.cpyu.org), Group Magazine's ministryandmedia.com, and neoscosmos.com. Periodic visits to these sites will keep parents informed of what's happening in their teenagers' world.

Fourth, regularly raise their awareness of what's happening in the unique youth culture of your particular student population. From time to time, you'll want to schedule a parent meeting to pass on your observations about the world of their teenagers. Or send out a monthly e-mail to keep them informed. Include information on the latest slang, fashion trends, music and media favorites, concerns among local school administrators (sexual behaviors, drugs of choice, and so on), attitudes, values, and behaviors. Again, they can't respond unless they know the reality.

And lastly, teach parents how to help their kids develop skills for evaluating everything they see and hear in pop culture through the filter of God's Word. Music and media are pervasive in the lives of children and teenagers. The emerging generation is the most media-savvy and media-saturated generation of all time. I recommend that you survey your students on their music and media tastes every three or four months. You can download and use the extensive survey posted on the CPYU site at www.cpyu.org/pageview.asp?pageid=13210 or develop a survey of your own. Tabulate the results to get a good picture of what your students are listening to, watching, and using. Then go to those media outlets yourself to get a sense of what your kids are learning about how to live as a teenager in today's world. Listen to the songs. Tune in to the radio stations. Play the video games. View the films. Watch the television shows. Use the Web sites already mentioned to access more information and reviews.

Your next step is to let the parents know where and how their kids are spending their media time along with what they're learning while they're there. Remember, you're equipping those "primary" missionaries to know the reality so they can respond.

Finally, teach parents and students to respond as Christians to their media culture by using CPYU's "3D Guide: How to Use Your Head to Guard Your Heart" media evaluation tool (more info at www.cpyu.org) together. This is a valuable way to help parents help their teenagers wade through the powerful, life-shaping messages coming through loud and clear in their media world.

Your job is to be part of an army of people who are determined to learn as much as they can about today's rapidly changing youth culture so they'll be effective cross-cultural missionaries…and just as effective at getting those funny looks.

Walt Mueller is the founder and president of the Center for Parent/Youth Understanding. A veteran of more than 30 years in youth ministry, he writes and speaks extensively on today's emerging generations and their culture. He's the author of Understanding Today's Youth Culture, *a husband, and father of four children…all of them either in or through their teenage years. You can learn more about CPYU at www.cpyu.org.*

Excellence in Parenting Certificate.

This is to certify that

Dan and Nancy Eaves

have demonstrated
excellence in parenting in seeing

Stacy

through many years
to adulthood.

Congratulations on a job well done!"

6

ENCOURAGING PARENTS
IN THEIR PARENTING

POSITIVE PROFILES

Nothing is more affirming for parents than to know that someone else thinks their kids are great. To send this positive message to the parents in your church, create a scrapbook "profile" of each student in your group.

To start, you'll need to come up with a few positive characteristics of each student (yes, for some of them, this will be difficult). Then find some scrapbook-quality paper and pens or markers. If you want to, you can also dig up a few photos of each person. And if you really want to go all out, find someone who's really into scrapbooking and see if you can get a lesson in designing really cool scrapbook pages (and finding the right supplies at a craft store).

Once you have your positive characteristics and your plans, create a short scrapbook (four or five pages) for each student in your group. Use the scrapbook to profile positive traits about that student. When the scrapbooks are finished, give them to parents as an affirmation of what they've built into their kids.

PARENTING ADVICE

Use this idea to compile parenting advice from a unique perspective—the perspective of your students.

During a youth meeting, ask teenagers to share some parenting advice—stuff they'd really like their parents to know. Encourage them to take this seriously and to share what they really want and need from their parents—and what they don't want and need. As they share, have a couple of adult helpers take notes on sheets of newsprint.

When students have finished sharing advice, ask them to talk about the great things they appreciate about their parents. Encourage them to focus both on who their parents are and on what they do for their kids.

After the meeting, compile all the advice and affirmations. Make copies for all the parents of students in your group. These booklets might contain the best parenting advice they'll ever receive!

WHAT IS QT?

I had said it many times to parents: "You need to spend quality time with your kids." I would send out ideas for quality time and had even begun to call it QT. "Have you had QT with your kids today?" I would herald the value of quality time and try to help parents not to confuse it with quantity time ("Just being in the same house as your teenager *isn't* quality time," I would say). This was all well and good, I suppose, but my ideas all changed one day while riding in a pickup truck in the middle of nowhere.

I was riding with the father of three of my youth group kids, and we began chatting about parenting and the skills involved in being a successful father. Naturally I launched into my QT philosophy with typical vigor and conviction. This father of three boys, in his typical abrupt but sincere style, interrupted me, saying, "You know, there really isn't quality time without quantity time."

I sat stunned. And I listened. He went on to explain to me a principle of parenting that I have since applied not only in raising my own children but also in talking to my youth parents as well. Quality time rarely happens by design. It is nearly impossible, especially with teenagers, to say, "I am going out to be with my son, and we are going to share and have quality time." Quality time hits at unexpected moments: a car ride home from school, a walk down to the soccer field, a few minutes washing dishes. I learned that day that quality time, especially for teenagers, usually happens consistently only if parents are around enough to be there when the quality moment hits. Sometimes it can be arranged, but I wonder at the amount of frustration I caused parents by implying they could arrange or manipulate quality time with their kids. Sure it can happen, but I am now convinced that quality time usually comes through quantity time. So instead of talking about just QT, I talk about QT = QT, *Quantity Time = Quality Time.*

YOUR DIPLOMA

Often youth ministries overlook the parents of graduates and their particular needs. While the student may be moving out of your program, his or her parents may be going through one of the great crises of their lives—sending a child away to college or into independent life. This is a chance to continue to care for your students' families as they experience the "empty nest" and to say thanks.

Print out "Excellence in Parenting" certificates. They might read, "This is to certify that _____ has demonstrated excellence in parenting in seeing _____ through many years to adulthood. Congratulations on a job well done!" Design these to look like a real degree with a gold seal (you can download images from the Internet), and put them on card stock.

Mail these out in large envelopes around the time of graduation, when everyone is celebrating the accomplishments of the student.

MOTHER'S DAY CARDS WITH A DIFFERENCE

Lots of parents feel insecure about their parenting. They worry about whether they are good enough and are getting it right. If your child grows up to be a well-adjusted adult who still enjoys a relationship with you, then as a parent you know that you must have done something right. But by then it's too late to do anything differently if your child doesn't turn out OK!

Use Mother's Day or Father's Day as an opportunity to tell parents what you appreciate about them. Send them cards, and write inside something like this: "You probably don't expect to get a card from a youth worker on Mother's/Father's Day, but I just wanted to say…" Tell them what you enjoy about their sons and daughters and what they contribute to the group. Thank them for the support they give you in your work. If you know them well enough, say what you appreciate about their parenting. Be sincere in what you say—don't embellish just to make them feel better, because they'll see right through that!

POSTCARDS FROM CAMP

When you take young people away for a camp, you probably encourage them to keep in touch with their parents, even if it's just to let them know they arrived safely. Next time you're at a camp with your group, send postcards home to teenagers' parents from you! Thank them for letting you spend the week with their sons and daughters. Make a point of sharing one constructive contribution that each parent's son or daughter has made to the camp. Tell parents what you hope to achieve during the camp, and maybe give them a specific prayer request so they know they have something to contribute to the camp apart from paying for it! Time is always short at a camp, so take the postcards with stamps and addresses already written on them, but make sure you write them while you're there so they are authentic.

PEER EYE FOR THE OLD GUYS

Before your regularly scheduled youth meeting time, enlist the help of an extra cameraperson to help you videotape this activity. When students arrive, ask them to sit in a circle and explain why each of their classmates totally rocks. Organize it in such a way that every person is complimented at least two or three times by peers.

After the session, have a copy of the video made for each student's parents so they can appreciate the good thoughts shared about their child. In addition to making students feel good, parents will gain a new respect as they see their teenager through the eyes of a young peer.

QUARTERLY CONFERENCES—YOUTH GROUP STYLE

News flash: If you're a 20-something youth leader with no kids or with very young children, nobody wants your advice on how to parent teenagers. Why? *Because you look like one of the least-qualified people on the planet.*

Don't take it personally—but do realize the credibility gap is there should you decide to share your thoughts on child rearing with parents of students in your ministry.

When you find yourself tempted to give parenting advice, count to 10 and walk away. Don't give advice—*ever.* At least, not out loud. Instead, hold quarterly conferences with parents. The schools do it, so the concept isn't foreign. And when schools invite parents to talk with teachers, the agenda is clear: Parents find out how their kids are doing.

Do the same thing, but forgo feedback about math skills. Rather, report to parents about their teenager's leadership skills, spiritual maturity, and faith development. Parents are hungry for that sort of information and seldom hear it.

Become the voice that provides thoughtful feedback about teenagers, and you'll have the ears of parents. You'll meet a need parents may not even be able to articulate until you address it.

Prayerfully prepare an assessment of each teenager in your group (ask your sponsors to help, if necessary), taking care to give specific examples to support your observations. Provide parents with suggestions on how you can come alongside them in encouraging their kids to stand strong in the faith and grow in their relationship with Jesus.

And through it all, provide support, not advice. Be a facilitator and servant, not an expert, and soon you'll find your words valued and sought after.

WHY SHOULD I GO TO CHURCH?

Sound familiar? How do parents answer their kids when they ask why they have to go to church? Be sure their response conveys the right message. Here are some responses to avoid—and a recommended response for the next time parents are challenged:

- "Christians are supposed to go to church." If kids see any part of their Christian experience as an obligation rather than a response from the heart, they'll choose not to take part in that activity.
- "Our family has been attending church for generations." You're not a Christian just because you're born into a Christian home. Allow your teenagers to see Christianity as a conscious choice rather than a cultural inheritance.
- "It's a great time to see your friends." Social life is a bonus to church attendance, not a substitute for spiritual motivations.
- "You'll go to church because we say so." It's better to encourage your kids to make it their own choice so they'll choose church when you don't have the "say so."

Recommended response: "We go to church because we choose to accept God's invitation to worship and fellowship with other believers."

(Adapted from Group Magazine, September/October 2002)

CRITICAL CARE FOR PARENTS

To minister to parents, invite them to come once a month to your youth ministry's Sunday night meeting. On these Sunday nights, parents and teenagers will start off together with devotions, video clips, or something else that's tied to the issue you'll be discussing.

Afterward, teenagers will go to their small groups for prayer, accountability, and discussion questions on that night's topic. Parents will head off to the

Critical Parents' Report (C.P.R.) for prayer, accountability, and discussion on the very same topic as their children. In the parents group, gear every discussion toward ideas they can utilize within their families. Then encourage teenagers and their parents to carry on the discussion after they get home.

(Adapted from Group Magazine, May/June 2004)

FAMILY RETREAT

Because a strong family foundation is so essential to a successful transition to adulthood, offer a biennial retreat that includes each student's family members.

The retreat should give students and their parents the opportunity to spend extended time together outside of their usual hyperbusy schedules. Include team-building activities, family interaction, and teaching that helps families prepare for the challenges of adolescence.

Offer activities for younger siblings, and cover the retreat cost for any high school–age family members who help run the children's program.

(Adapted from Group Magazine, March/April 2004)

FAMILY 14-ER

As you begin planning for the year ahead, consider designating a two-week period as The Family 14, a time when your youth ministry highlights activities that get families eating, working, playing, and praying together.

Plan special outings such as family trips to a recreation center, amusement park, or sports event. Bring in family-oriented speakers or entertainers, have a family picnic or dinner, and hold a family game night. Sponsor a local mission project for families to work on. Bring families together for a special worship service.

(Adapted from Group Magazine, September/October 2003)

ENCOURAGING PARENTS…SO SIMPLE, YET SO VITAL!
BY KURT JOHNSTON

I'm the parent of two children, and I've learned something: Parenting is tough stuff, and my kids are only in elementary school! Throughout my ministry career, I've learned that most of my parent problems don't stem from mean-spirited, distrusting parents who are out to ruin my group but rather from parents who truly love their kids and are doing their best to raise them into Christlike young men and women.

No one has ever accused me of being an intellectual. I tend to believe the simplest approach to dilemmas is often the best. With this disclaimer firmly in place, let me give you what I believe is the simplest and most effective way to minister to the parents of your students. *Encourage them!*

Right about now you may be thinking, "Kurt, you are not only a nonintellectual, but you are just downright dumb! Certainly you've learned more about ministering to parents over the years than that." Yeah, I've learned a lot…I've read a lot…I've attended workshops a lot…and I've even written a lot. But at the end of the day, I'm convinced that many parents of teenagers are at their wits' end and grasping at straws. They're dying for somebody, anybody, to breathe a little encouragement into them, to let them know things are going be OK. That's where we can come in! Most youth workers haven't yet navigated the waters on raising teenagers, so it's a little unrealistic to present ourselves as experts on the topic. However, all of us are capable of being cheerleaders for parents and looking for ways, however small, to encourage them.

Here are a few simple but effective ways I've been able to encourage parents in my ministry at Saddleback:

• **Open-door policy**—Let parents know that they are always welcome to pop into your youth ministry program. Encourage them to stick around once in a while so they know what their students are learning in church and what your program is all about.

- **Parent newsletter**—An oldie but goodie! Send out a monthly newsletter that points parents to Web sites and articles about parenting. Put a few fun quips and quotes to make 'em chuckle.

- **Easy access**—The more your ministry grows, the busier you get. Parents are often frustrated when they can't track down an answer to a question. If they have a concern, they expect someone to return their phone call. Let parents know your office hours, return phone calls and e-mails promptly, and do your best to be accessible.

- **Help them prioritize**—In our busy culture, church often becomes another plate to juggle. In fact, if your youth group is like mine, you become lots of plates for families to juggle because you offer so much. Each month, on your Web site or in your newsletter, list all the programs and activities your ministry is doing that month, and give some commentary as to the purpose of the event and whom you hope to target (for example, bowling night is for our small groups to connect with each other). This will help families select their church events for the month.

- **Random acts of kindness**—There are endless little acts of kindness you and your team can do for parents that will let them know you're thinking of them. Show up at their house with a plant or some flowers. Cook a dinner to drop off at their house on a night when they're too busy to cook. Mail them a couple of movie passes for their date nights. The list goes on and on. Make little cards that say something like "The youth ministry at church is praying for you!" and leave them at the scene of your Random Act.

- **Random phone calls**—My favorite…probably because it's the simplest. Take one hour a week in the evening to randomly call several parents. Brag on their kids, thank them for supporting your ministry, and pray for them.

Kurt Johnston is the junior high pastor at Saddleback Church in Southern California. In ministry since 1988, Kurt is also a sought-after speaker and writer on ministry to young teenagers. Kurt is married to Rachel, and they have two children, Kayla and Cole.

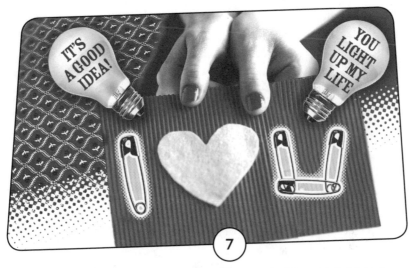

HELPING KIDS RESPECT, HONOR, AND LOVE THEIR PARENTS

SECRET MISSION

Give teenagers secret missions that could transform their family lives.

Tell teenagers you're giving them a secret mission. Assign them the task of secretly finding out five things their parents would just love—or maybe they already know. These might be gifts their parents would love to receive, things their parents would like someone to do for them, places their parents would love to go, or other special things.

Once youth have their five ideas, challenge them to find sneaky ways to give these five things to their parents. They might do them all at once or spread out these special things over time.

Let teenagers know they can enlist each other's help as necessary. Give them plenty of time to accomplish this mission (at least a couple of months).

After their assignments are complete (or while they are in process), discuss them with teenagers. Talk about what effect these special things have on their parents—and especially on their relationships with their parents.

BIOGRAPHY

For this activity, have students "swap parents." Find out which parents in your group would be willing to participate in this experience. Then assign each of those parents to a couple of teenagers who can work together to interview him or her.

Once teenagers know the identities of their assigned parents, charge youth with the task of writing biographies about those parents. To do so, they'll need to set up some time to do at least one interview with their assigned parents. Encourage them to ask the parents questions about their lives, focusing especially on what the parents experienced when they were teenagers. Here are some suggested questions:

- How old are you?
- When and where were you born?
- What's your favorite food? TV show? hobby?
- If you could go on vacation anywhere in the world, where would you go?
- When you were 7 years old, what did you want to be when you grew up?
- What was your first job?
- Where did you go to high school?
- When you were a teenager, what made you feel happiest?
- When you were a teenager, when did you feel loneliest?
- What was your relationship with your parents like when you were a teenager?
- What is one story you remember from when you were in 10th grade?
- What is one thing you wish your teenager knew about you?

When students have completed their interviews, have them write biographies of their assigned parents. When the biographies are complete, give them to the parents' kids. Encourage teenagers to talk about these biographies with their parents.

PARENT POLL

Use this creative idea to help teenagers minister to their parents on an ongoing basis.

Conduct a poll among parents to find out what they would really like their kids to do to show they love their parents—from cleaning their rooms to sending them on a cruise. You can include this survey in a parent newsletter, send it out in an e-mail, or distribute it after a meeting.

Once you receive your completed surveys, collect the ideas in a notebook (it would be helpful to indicate which ideas were the most popular among parents). Keep the notebook in your office or in the youth room—someplace where students can refer to it often.

Encourage teenagers to look through the ideas regularly to find ideas they can try on their parents. Every now and then, pull out the notebook during a youth meeting and encourage each person to choose something he or she can do to surprise his or her parents.

DON'T GET SMART! GET WISE!

Try this Bible study from the book of Proverbs to show your youth some practical advice about listening to their parents.

Start by breaking your students into groups of no more than five. Provide for them the definition of a *proverb*: a brief, memorable saying that provides wise instruction for life. You may want to provide them with a few examples, such as "A penny saved is a penny earned" or "As water reflects a face, so a man's heart reflects the man" (Proverbs 27:19).

Give each group paper and pens or pencils, and instruct groups to come up with some wise proverbs for each of the following topics. Encourage students to think creatively. The proverbs can be funny or serious.

- Making a perfect dinner ("Macaroni and cheese and nothing else is a meal fit for a king.")
- Arranging the perfect date
- Succeeding in school
- Staying friends
- Living with parents

Give the students some time to work on their proverbs and then have them share them with the rest of the groups.

Ask:

- **What was it like to write proverbs? Was it easy or difficult? Why?**
- **What is the value of putting wisdom in the form of proverbs?**

Say: **The Bible has a whole book of proverbs (appropriately called Proverbs) that offers advice for successful living—advice about friendship, the words you use, serving God, and, yes, dealing with your parents. It's this last topic that we want to focus on today.**

Turn in your Bibles to the book of Proverbs, and scan the following verses: 1:8; 1:15; 2:1; 3:1; 3:11; 4:1; 4:20; and 5:1.

Ask:

- **What word is repeated in each of those verses?** (Son.)
- **Why would the writer have addressed the book of Proverbs to a son?**

(Note that the writer may have been addressing his own son but also addressing all "sons," meaning all young people.)

• **What is the value of learning wisdom while you are young?**

Say: **Let's go back and focus on 1:8-9; 3:1-2; and 5:1-2.**

Have someone read each of the above passages.

Ask:

• **What similar advice is given in each of these verses?**

• **What are the different results that come from following this advice, according to the different sections?**

• **Why is it sometimes hard to listen to our parents' counsel?**

• **Why would the Bible, particularly in these verses, be so adamant about us doing so? What are the benefits?**

• **Can someone share about a time you either followed your parents' wishes and were glad or did not follow your parents' wishes and regretted it? Tell about it.**

In closing, you may want to ask your students to explore the book of Proverbs to find other verses that give them advice regarding how they should relate to their parents (and how their parents should relate to them!).

IN THEIR SHOES

Have your students get pictures of their parents when they were teenagers. Gather the students to share and discuss the pictures. Ask what they think life was like for their parents back then. What challenges did they face? What was the same about being a teenager as it is now?

Give students a list of seven or more questions that a teenager could ask his or her parents about the parents' own teenage years. These could include descriptions of hobbies and activities, family life, and personal challenges. Have your students ask their parents one of the questions each day.

Gather the students again after a week of asking questions. Discuss what they learned, and let them tell their parents' stories. Then lead a discussion of the similarities and differences of teenage life then and today. Ask students if they have a sense for the fact that their parents went through the normal struggles people go through when they grow up. Challenge students to tell their parents what they appreciate about them when they return the photographs.

WEARING OUT THE THANKS

Young people wear T-shirt slogans to make all kinds of statements. Parents don't always want to see those statements. Here is a chance to make a T-shirt statement every parent will want to see: "Dear parent, thank you!" Youth can never wear out thanks to their parents. But with this T-shirt, this statement of thanks can be worn out—that is, out on the town.

Have each teenager bring one plain white T-shirt for each of his or her parents to a youth meeting. Provide black markers, and have them write large statements of thanks on the fronts of the T-shirts. On the backs of the shirts, have them list 10 things they appreciate about their parents. Encourage them to be creative in their designing. Before they leave, have the youth commit to wearing their T-shirts out for one day.

On that day, they should set aside some time to spend with their parents and explain their T-shirts. At the end of the sharing, they should say a prayer of thanks with their parents. Have the youth report back to the group their experience with their parents. Thank them for their efforts in wearing out the thanks.

R-E-S-P-E-C-T

Parents don't always get the respect and love they deserve. Here are five wonderful ways to make sure they get more r-e-s-p-e-c-t. Youth will obligate themselves to five selfless acts of service to an overjoyed parent.

This promising idea involves youth creating "Luv Coupons" for a parent to redeem. At a youth meeting, give each teenager five blank index cards and a pen or pencil. Have each teenager use his or her artistic flair to create five Luv Coupons. Have teenagers create one coupon for each of the following subjects:

- a chore
- a favor
- a promise to stop a bad habit
- a promise to begin a good habit
- a wild card (parent's choice of any of the above)

Have the youth take the coupons home and give them to their parents. Encourage teenagers to take that moment to remind their parents that they really do love and respect them. The words will be a nice step toward showing love and respect. The coupons will be a great leap in that direction. Parents rejoice!

BEFORE YOU WERE BORN: PARENTS TELL THEIR STORIES

In order to help parents and their teenagers have a better relationship, encourage parents to tell their personal stories to their teenagers. Some teenagers have only heard their parents' stories contextualized within "When I was your age, I never thought of asking my parent if I could see a band like that!" Rather than an anecdote to teach a lesson, a story can lead a teenager to learn more about his or her parent and respect, honor, and love the parent more.

Encourage parents to take a few hours over several weekends to type (or write, if they're more comfortable doing that) their life stories. Give them some questions to prompt their writing:

- How did I get to where I am today?
- What have been my main priorities in life? How have I demonstrated this?
- What has my spiritual journey been like?
- What regrets do I have? How have I learned from my mistakes?
- What things have I done that I'm still very excited about?
- How has my origin affected who I am today?

A completed story (or several vignettes, at least) can be a very special gift to a teenager. Rather than just handing it to them, reading it aloud will make the story more personal. Even if the parent gets teary reading difficult memories aloud, his or her vulnerability will help the teenager realize the humanity of his or her parent.

PRETEND TO BE A PARENT

When you're young, it's very easy to take your parents for granted. Your dirty clothes somehow end up back in your closet nice and clean, there's food on the table regularly, the garden gets weeded, the house gets cleaned, and your bed gets changed without you having to lift a finger! When you leave home and have to do all these things for yourself, you suddenly appreciate just how much work your parents put into looking after you.

Challenge your young people to have a "pretend to be a parent" Saturday. They should think of three things that their moms and dads always do for them and the family—maybe cleaning the house, shopping for food, working in the garden, cooking a meal, or washing the car. Then they should take on those three chores and do them to the best of their ability. Having to do what your mom or dad normally does for you is a great way to appreciate and respect them while you're still at home, rather than taking them for granted!

GROOVY!

Ready to party? Deck the walls with funky décor from days gone by for a rockin' "Decades" party.

Create invitations beforehand, inviting students and their parents to the bash of the century. They should come in costume—students dressed in apparel their parents might have worn in high school, parents dressed as modern-day teenagers! Encourage parents to bring old yearbooks along for some laughs.

Help the generations bond by initiating a "Top That" story contest where partygoers try to outdo one another with funny stories from their younger years.

Have some great retro tunes on hand. Don't forget to see who can copy the best John Travolta dance moves. Be forewarned—your students have no idea who John Travolta is.

HEARTS ARE WHERE THE HOME IS

Undeniably, the best valentine is a homemade valentine. Use this fun card-making activity to add smiles to your youth's Valentine's Day.

The youth group meeting before Valentine's Day, set out basic supplies for making valentines: red, pink, and white card stock; markers; glue; tape; and scissors. Also set out household items that could contribute to an unusual valentine. You might choose some of the following: an empty soft drink can, nail polish, dryer sheets or lint, toothpaste, grass clippings, toilet paper, tea bags, twist ties, safety pins, socks, or a burned-out light bulb. Prepare three slips of scrap paper for each teenager, writing on each slip one of the household items you set out.

Then tell youth they will be creating valentines for their parents. Mix up the slips of paper, and have everyone choose three slips. Each person must use those three items in the construction of his or her valentine.

Have youth take their completed cards home. They can present their valentines to their parents and spend time with them on Valentine's Day.

(Adapted from Group Magazine, January/February 2004)

HONOR AND BLESSING

It's the job of children to honor their parents, and it's the job of parents to bless their children. Use this activity based on Ephesians 6:1-4 from *Confirming Your Faith* by Jim Burns (Group Publishing, Inc.) to close your next parent-teenager meeting or event:

Students—Have teenagers each write a statement of honor for their parents, spelling out the following: those things that they most appreciate, the guidance they know they still need, and the things they're committed to doing to love and honor their parents.

Parents—Have parents each write out a blessing for their children that includes the following: those things they most appreciate about their children, what they're proud about, and what they commit to doing to faithfully pass on their Christian faith.

Have each family come together to share what they've written. Then have them offer a prayer like this one (or use their own words):

Students—"God, thank you for my parent(s). I acknowledge your part in bringing our family together. I want to honor my parent(s) and with your help become a more obedient child of God and obey my parent(s) through these important years. Thank you for my dad because _____. Thank you for my mom because _____. Please bless our family and help us to be as Christ-honoring as possible. In the name of Jesus, amen."

Parents—"God, thank you for _____. I acknowledge your part in bringing our family together and thank you for bringing_____ into our lives. Thank you for _____ because _____. Help me to be the parent you want me to be. Please bless our family and help us to honor Christ in every part of our lives. In the name of Jesus, amen."

(Adapted from Group Magazine, November/December 2003)

PARENTS IN PRINT

Affirm parents and help their teenagers see them through new eyes with this easy-to-pull-off interview project.

Have your youth group members form interview teams, and give each team a list of three or four parents. Have all the teenagers brainstorm a series of interview questions such as "What's the hardest job you ever had?" "How is your teenager's life most different from your own life as a teenager?" and "What does God look like when you picture him in your mind?"

Schedule prearranged times for teams to meet with individual youth group parents for 20 to 30 minutes. Have teenagers divide their interview duties so all team members actively participate. Make sure at least one young person on each team serves as the recorder.

After the interviews have been completed and notes organized, have teams work with your church's newsletter editor to write up the interviews. Publish the interviews over time, highlighting parents as valuable partners in teenagers' faith journeys.

(Adapted from Group Magazine, September/October 2002)

BRIDGE WORK

Would you like to start a conversation between parents and teenagers about their relationships with each other? Build a bridge.

Form two teams that each include parents and teenagers, but don't put parents and their children on the same team. You'll need cardboard, string, masking tape, and two tables. Place the tables ("mountains") 10 feet apart, and divide the space between them with a line of masking tape on the floor (the "great divide").

Each team will begin at one mountain and attempt to construct a half-bridge over the divide using its supplies of cardboard, string, and masking tape. The goal is for both teams to connect their bridges in the middle, making one bridge. Give everyone 30 to 45 minutes to construct the bridge without directly talking to each other. Every 5 or 10 minutes, pick one parent and his or her teenager to leave the room for a two-minute strategy meeting. Afterward, test the bridge's strength by placing a large object in the middle of the bridge to see if it holds.

Then ask:

- **What was most the challenging aspect of this activity? the most rewarding aspect?**
- **If you could have talked freely with each other, how would this experience have been different?**
- **What do you think is the biggest challenge in communicating with your parents or your teenagers?**
- **What are some of the "bridges" you use in those relationships?**
- **What are some bridges that you might need to build?**

(Adapted from Group Magazine, May/June 2002)

WRAP PARTY

Invite "couples" of one teenager and one parent to an end-of-the-year celebration, and help teenagers discover that their parents can be fun.

Create a festive event that includes food, games, and group interaction. Choose one discussion topic, and focus all the activities around this central theme.

For example, if you choose a topic such as spiritual gifts and natural talents, you might have parents and teenagers work together on a skit that illustrates how to use our gifts to live for God. A fun game might involve the talent of communication: Blindfold parents and instruct them to follow their children's directions to find water pistols and spray the opposite teams.

Not only will parents and kids have fun together, but parents will also experience interactive learning and get to know youth group leaders.

(Adapted from Group Magazine, May/June 2002)

THE ULTIMATE BALANCING ACT
BY JEANNE MAYO

When I started in youth ministry 35 exciting years ago, I made myself one simple promise: I was *not* going to be my own children's youth pastor. Sounds simple enough, doesn't it? But 35 years later and now being an official "empty nester" with my two adult sons out of the home, I smilingly tell you that I broke that promise to myself—*at my sons' request*—and I'm so very glad I did.

How well I remember the day my oldest son, Josh, sat me down for a serious talk. He was in fifth grade at the time and had overheard his father and me talking about my needing to move out of the youth ministry "because our boys are almost there." That day, Josh changed my perspective in a way I had never imagined possible. He tearfully blurted out, "It's just not fair, Mom. It's just not fair. You've made the youth ministry great for everyone else and now you're going to ditch out on Justin and me. You just can't do that to us!"

That was the wake-up call I needed. It *was* possible to be both a youth pastor and a parent to teenagers who were in the group. Not only was it possible, but it became one of the most fulfilling seasons of my ministry. Obviously, it was often the balancing act of the century, but it was worth every bit of energy I sent in that direction. Allow me to share with you some of the keys to navigating this era in my spiritual journey:

1. I privately talked to a couple of my finest volunteer leaders in the group and asked them to each "own" one of my sons during these years. You see, I realize that all teenagers need what I call "a third voice" (dad, mom, and a third influential person). So I chose a different leader for each of my two sons—someone I had faith in and someone whose personality I felt would be a great match for my boy. Though I asked them to *never reveal this request to either of my sons,* I explained that I wanted my boys to have someone they could trust and look up to besides their dad and me. I also asked a couple of sharp high school guys to "be cool" to my sons when they entered the youth group as middle school students. I knew that those connections would make my sons feel like a million bucks while giving them the sense that they had key people to talk with in the youth group besides just me. These connections became huge.

2. I made a personal commitment to never, ever use the youth meeting as a forum for "getting a message to my sons." Teenagers are smart. I knew my sons would know if I was trying to "get them told" through a point in my message. So I made sure that I handled family and personal concerns personally. I also never sought my kids out in the youth gathering. If they wanted me, they came to me. I made sure they had their own turf.

3. I often asked my sons for their advice regarding the youth group. I made them feel like partners in the journey, and whenever possible, I tried to implement some of their suggestions.

4. I worked hard to make sure my sons never felt in competition with the youth group. Granted, this sometimes took pretty fierce time management. But I made sure I verbalized enough love and spent enough personal time that my sons knew where they rated.

5. Along the journey, I occasionally had private talks with both of my sons to see if I was doing anything that made them feel awkward or that they wanted changed. One time my youngest son, Justin, told me that my shoes on Wednesday night embarrassed him. Another time, Josh told me he preferred my never mentioning his name from the front when I told a story about our family. Granted, I always held my breath, thinking I would get more serious adjustments. But my idea was that I wanted to know anything—big or small—that made this arrangement awkward for them as we made the journey together. (By the way, I bought some new shoes!)

6. I never, ever told a story in the youth group that referred to our family without first getting my sons' approval. It's important that your children still feel that their *personal life* is their *personal life*…no matter how great the story is.

7. When my sons showed interest in an area of ministry, I worked overtime to support them in that interest. No, I didn't "play favorites." But behind the scenes, I felt very comfortable making sure my sons had everything necessary to grow in the ministry arenas that started to catch their hearts. I call this "loading the bases for the Holy Spirit's success."

8-10. (Three points combined because this is the "big one") I scheduled, planned, and worked overtime to make sure I was "a parent who was also a youth pastor"…not "a youth pastor who was also a parent." What's that mean? I just made sure my two sons didn't get the emotional leftovers. I fought to be at every soccer game, every parent night, and every other function at which my sons needed to have a mom—both public and private. During those years, it was not rare for me to decline speaking to several thousand teenagers because I saw one of my son's varsity soccer games conflicted with that date. The result? The Mayo boys didn't grow up resenting the ministry. Even more important, they didn't grow up resenting the God of the ministry.

The ultimate compliment was paid to me on the afternoon my youngest son was graduating from the university. While sitting through the commencement exercises, waiting for his name to be called, he wrote me a thank you note that he snuck into my hands later that afternoon. It read, "Dear Mom, As I graduate from the university today, I wanted to write you a note and say 'thank you' for being the best mom in the whole world." He filled the card with heartwarming memories. But his closing sentence was the clincher. It read, "P.S. By the way, Mom, thanks for always keeping the ministry your side job."

Pretty powerful sentence, don't you think? It's a balancing act to be both a youth pastor and parent of a teenager. But if you keep the youth ministry your side job, the end results will be overwhelmingly fulfilling.

Jeanne Mayo has been in full-time local youth ministry for over three decades. Her youth ministries have been as large as 1,000 students on a weekly basis. She is now the youth pastor at a church in Atlanta, where her husband recently accepted a pastorate. She travels internationally to speak and is the president of Youth Source, a mentoring and coaching ministry to youth leaders. Find them on the Web at www.youthsource.com.

8

GROWING YOUR ADULT VOLUNTEERS

Before this idea, check with some other local youth workers to make sure they're open to having your volunteers visit.

At a volunteer meeting, present the idea of volunteers visiting other youth ministry programs to see how they operate and possibly to gain ideas on how your church can minister more effectively. Tell volunteers which churches have expressed interest in having them visit, and allow volunteers to set up these "snoop trips" when it's convenient for them. Give them a deadline, though (a month or two), so they can get together and discuss their experiences with you. Suggest the volunteers visit groups individually, in pairs, or in very small groups to avoid disrupting the other groups' atmospheres with their presence.

Here are some things your volunteers can observe during their experiences:

• What types of teenagers does this church seem to attract?
• How would you describe this youth ministry's "personality"?
• What is the main emphasis of this youth ministry?

- What kind of activities does this youth group do?
- What creative ideas does this youth ministry use?

A month or two later, hold another volunteer meeting to discuss the volunteers' experiences. Talk about what kinds of changes you might want to make in your ministry as a result of what they saw and experienced.

VOLUNTEER CHARADES

Use this fun idea to bring volunteers closer to one another—and to discover how to minister to them more effectively.

At a volunteer meeting, have your volunteers play a game of Charades to discuss their experiences as volunteers. Tell them you'll ask a question and they'll have to use Charades to answer it. You can either have one person answer a question or ask everyone to address each question.

Ask questions such as these:
- What was our funniest youth group moment?
- Who is the funniest student in the group?
- What has been your most rewarding youth ministry moment?
- What's your most outrageous van or bus story?
- What's been the most entertaining youth group romance?
- What's been your greatest youth ministry disaster?
- What is your biggest youth ministry fear?

You'll probably get some hilarious results. You'll probably also gain insights into what makes your team tick and how you can help each other in ministry.

THE KIDS AREN'T LOOKING

Sometimes one of the best gifts a leader can give his or her team is to spend time with them. Your team may have learned significant things about ministry from you and may want nothing more than to spend some leisure time together.

Plan a barbecue and pool party (someone from the church might sponsor it for you) for your leadership team and parents. The theme of the party is "The Kids Aren't Looking!" Allow time just to play and get to know one another. At some point, gather everyone for a discussion of stunts they tried to get away with when they were teenagers and what they think of the teenage culture today. Remember, this isn't for the sake of business; it's just to share ideas. There is no to-do list when the conversation is over. A fun question to ask parents is "What's the first thing you want to do once your kids move out of the house?"

TEAMING WITH PRIDE

Ask not what your youth can do for you, but ask what you can do for your youth. This is a message that really resonates when youth volunteers are recognized and appreciated. This is a potent tool for giving your team of youth volunteers some genuine pride in what they do.

Present your team of youth volunteers to the church while recognizing their contributions of time and love. When volunteers understand that their efforts make a difference, they will be encouraged to continue their support. When parents and others see the benefits of volunteering, they will be inspired to join the team.

Work with church leaders to establish a yearly service to recognize youth volunteers. In preparation for this service, invite the volunteers to the special service. Have teenagers use card stock and colored markers to prepare one thank you card for each volunteer. The card should be personalized with the volunteer's name. Each card should have symbols or drawings that represent that individual's contributions.

At the service, invite the volunteers to the front of the church and give them their thank you cards. Select three youth to share with the congregation what having the volunteers means to the youth group and what it means to them personally. Make some closing comments, and invite parents and others to share in the meaningful experience of volunteering. Go team!

GET THE BOOT: LEADERSHIP BOOT CAMP

Parents and volunteers associated with a youth group often change from year to year. How can these changing but important leaders work well together and minister effectively? A yearly retreat designed to draw the group together and develop some basic ministry skills is a boot in the right direction. Invite your volunteers and parents of the youth to an annual "Leadership Boot Camp."

Pick an inspiring location and an available weekend. Consider adding the following elements to your programming:

- Review of the previous year's programs—Discuss the strengths and weaknesses of each.
- A guest speaker—Invite an experienced youth leader to address ministry skills. While the youth leader is certainly qualified, the idea of a "guest" sparks interest.
- Personal sharing and testimony—Ask the group to prepare for this element in advance.
- Bible study—Focus on Christ's ministry, and have the study for one hour after every meal.

- Prayer—Be creative and practice a variety of prayer methods.
- Commitment—Challenge the group to be leaders within and without the youth group.
- Recreation—Choose challenging activities that involve team building.
- Personal time—Set aside time in the morning and evening for individuals to have personal time with God.

Your volunteers and parents of your youth will be much more effective ministers and more confident leaders when they have experienced a Leadership Boot Camp. It can be a lot of work, but it's a great deal for them and your youth. Go leaders!

YOU ROCK!

Making volunteers feel appreciated is an essential part of successful ministry. Use this idea to publicly recognize the contributions and good qualities of those who donate their time—the one who faithfully puts all the chairs and tables away after youth group or the one who always has a smile for every teenager, even the morning after a sleepless lock-in.

VOLUNTEER OF THE MONTH
THANKS FOR DRIVING THE MINISTRY.

Select a traveling trophy to award at your staff meeting each month to an outstanding volunteer. Be creative when selecting the trophy. For example, you could buy a steering wheel and hand it to the volunteer who has been most responsible for "driving" the ministry that month. Encourage each awardee to decorate or sign or otherwise improve the trophy before it is awarded to the next person. Another idea is to use a Bible or devotion book for your trophy and encourage each awardee to mark his or her favorite verses or devotions with a personal note.

Soon the awarding of the traveling trophy will be the highlight of your staff meetings. Your volunteers will never want to miss a meeting!

DISHCLOTHS AND ROAD MAPS

Invite all your adult volunteers to a meal. Ask them to think in advance about these two questions: How do I feel about the youth group at the moment? What are my dreams for the youth group? Invite them to bring to the meal two things that represent their answers, one for each of those questions. For example, someone who is not feeling very positive about their involvement might bring along a dishcloth because helping in the youth group feels like a bit of a chore. Someone else might bring along a map because his or her dream is to be able to give direction to young people for their lives. Eat the meal, enjoy each other's company, and relax together. Then over dessert, invite everyone in turn to explain what he or she has brought and why. This activity can provoke interesting conversation and help volunteers get to know each other better. Make sure you affirm people's contributions, both the positive and the negative comments. Make a note of anything that you will need to follow up on in the future.

SWAP MEET

Sharpen your group of adult volunteers and parents by encouraging quality time with teenagers other than their own. Organize a Sunday Lunch Swap in which volunteers and parents shake things up and treat teenagers in the youth group to Sunday lunch.

Coordinate with a restaurant ahead of time, and spend some thought pairing students with adults.

Travel to the restaurant in the church van or bus, and then encourage the lunch partners to spread out once you've arrived. To help them really get to know the people they've been assigned to, you may wish to provide several questions each pair should ask each other.

Debrief with parents and sponsors afterward, and pray for any special needs uncovered during lunchtime conversations.

PLUGGED IN

Take time at your monthly staff meeting to reward one of your volunteers with a unique gift—an extension cord.

Announce that you'd like to highlight an adult leader who has done a great job of helping plug kids in to Christ, and then present that person with a large extension cord. Be specific about what you've observed that led you to honor this particular volunteer. Then either have the person keep the extension cord as a permanent sign of encouragement, or have him or her keep it for one month, sign it, and then present it to another leader who's helping students get plugged in.

(Adapted from Group Magazine, March/April, 2004)

EXTRAORDINARY THANKS

Instead of writing ordinary thank you notes to your youth group volunteers and parents, here's a creative gift that people will love to use and show off.

Buy an inexpensive, white plastic tablecloth for each of the youth group's volunteers. Then have students write thank you messages on the tablecloths with paint markers, which are available at craft stores. Young people can add drawings that illustrate various aspects of the youth group and how the church members helped.

(Adapted from Group Magazine, November/December 2003)

UNUSUAL SUSPECTS

Empty nesters and senior adults in your church community may not be interested in a long-term commitment to youth ministry, but many would make ideal short-term youth group "missionaries."

Seek out temporary leaders with areas of expertise—for example, worship leaders, artists, counselors, or spiritual directors. Look for mentors who can share their experiences about developing a relationship with Jesus and becoming a person who's respected by others.

Be sure to have your long-term leaders engaged in working with the "missionaries." Students will love having their leaders learning alongside them, and the short-term leaders will appreciate having leaders present who support them and already know the teenagers.

(Adapted from Group Magazine, September/October 2003)

HAVE I TOLD YOU LATELY?

Teenagers often have a hard time saying thank you because they don't know how. Help them express gratitude to your adult leaders, who may sometimes feel they're doing a thankless job.

At least once a year, have an unannounced Leader Appreciation Night. For each youth leader, place a poster on the wall of your meeting room and attach a marker on a string. As students come in, tell them that they're free to write a note or message to the leaders on their respective posters. Encourage the adult leaders to add their notes to other leaders' posters, too.

If the size of your group permits, have each leader take a turn in a specially designated chair. While each leader is in the "hot seat," anyone can speak up and say something positive about that person. It might be a story about something fun that the leader did or about a way that the leader has shown care for someone.

At the end of the night, the teenagers walk away in high spirits because they were able to express themselves, and the leaders walk away realizing that the little things they do with the teenagers really do matter.

(Adapted from Group Magazine, September/October 2003)

PRAYER LIFT

You may have prayer warriors who are praying for the young people in your youth ministry, but have you considered recruiting prayer support for your adult leaders?

Enlist one or two church members to pray daily for a specific volunteer. Commission enough people so that all your volunteers are being prayed for. Encourage adult leaders and their prayer partners to connect briefly on Sunday mornings so adult leaders can pass along prayer requests and receive encouragement from their supporters.

Your volunteers will be uplifted by daily prayer—the most powerful tool in youth ministry.

(Adapted from Group Magazine, May/June 2003)

VOLUNTEER G.R.O.W.T.H.

It takes far less time and energy to nurture the volunteers you already have than it does to recruit new ones, so follow these suggestions for dynamic development:

Grace—Volunteers hunger for an unconditional working environment in which mistakes are made but not memorialized, errors are allowed but not announced, and failure isn't final or fatal. Encourage your adult volunteers to be creative and risky. Give them permission to mess up, and when they do, forgive and forget.

Relationships—Friendships are a primary need, and great youth ministries create strong bonds among the adult staffers. Invest time together apart from the kids—barbecue and bowl, party and play.

Ownership—The Lone Ranger lives in many youth ministries despite volunteers' desire to contribute creativity, abilities, and resources. The need to be needed is a deep one. Repent and let Tonto shake the sheriff's hand occasionally. Check out *No More Lone Rangers: How to Build a Team-Centered Youth Ministry* by David Chow (Group Publishing, Inc.).

Worth—Power is rooted in ownership, but purpose is planted in our contributions. It's not enough to grant permission for adult leaders to lead; we must also affirm and accentuate their passions and personalities. Encouragement and exhortation yield personal worth.

Training—Everybody craves success, and no one wants to be embarrassed, so provide training that enables your adult volunteers to lead with confidence.

Humor—Youth ministry is fun. That's a reason many of us can't get it out of our blood. Kids are hilarious. Camps and conferences are a hoot. Even our lessons are laced with laughter. And then there are staff meetings (OK, maybe not everything is funny!). So lighten up. It's OK to be serious, but don't forget to smile.

(Adapted from Group Magazine, March/April 2003)

KEEP IT "SMALL"

If your adult leaders sacrifice being in a small group to serve in the youth ministry, provide a small-group environment as part of your team meetings.

Begin meetings with a community-building time. Have each person bring a dish of food to share so everyone can eat and talk.

Utilize the second part of the meeting for ministry training on an area of need, such as counseling teenagers, understanding youth culture, or leading discussions. Include training on personal growth issues from time to time because leaders must be growing spiritually to effectively influence students.

During the last section of the meeting, have adult leaders form small groups based on their roles and the age groups they work with. Have groups discuss the training talk and how it applies to the students they shepherd. Have each small group address any housekeeping issues and then close by praying together.

(Adapted from Group Magazine, March/April 2003)

B.I.B.L.E. CHECK

Here's a quick and easy B.I.B.L.E. checklist to make sure you're motivating and involving your adult leaders:

Believe in them—When you believe that people can do the job, you're able to let go and give them ownership. Ownership breeds joy and long-term commitment.

Instruct them—We honor our adult leaders when we take the time to teach them about youth ministry.

Bring them along—Whenever you visit school campuses or attend teenagers' events, bring along one of your adult leaders. Going out "two by two" is a wonderful biblical model.

Love them—Jesus loved and spent time with his disciples, and we're called to do the same with our adult leaders.

Encourage them—Adult leaders are unlikely to receive words of appreciation or encouragement from teenagers. Write notes of encouragement to your volunteers, and take them out to lunch from time to time.

Periodically, do this B.I.B.L.E. check to make sure you're spending time building your ministry.

(Adapted from Group Magazine, November/December 2002)

VOLUNTEERS' VOLUNTEER

The nurturing and encouragement of volunteers is a critical part of any youth minister's success, but sometimes we simply forget to say thanks or we overlook those who are working behind the scenes. How can you prevent this? Recruit a volunteer to care for volunteers.

Give this person a budget to spend on flowers, cards, gifts, or thank you dinners. Commission the volunteer to help you create a culture of thanks and encouragement. And, as your ministry grows, include this person as part of your staff team—someday the director of volunteers may even become a paid staff member.

(Adapted from Group Magazine, May/June 2002)

VOLUNTEER YEAR

A volunteer calendar makes a great gift for your adult leaders, but it takes some long-term planning. So start taking photos now of your volunteers in action.

You'll need one great photo for each month. Focus on seasonal events as much as possible: a summer mission trip or fun day, the fall retreat, holiday activities, and so on.

You can either go the Kinko's route or use your computer to create the calendar. Calendar-making software is often included in basic software packages, it's available as part of publishing software such as Microsoft Publisher 2000, and it's also available on the Internet at sites such as www.famcal.com.

You can scan your photos, use a digital camera, or have your photos developed and placed on a CD. When you make the calendar, remember to note upcoming events and meetings on the appropriate dates.

(Adapted from Group Magazine, May/June 2001)

CONNECTING PARENTS IN A WORLD OF OUTSOURCING
BY STEVE ARGUE

We live in a world where, in just about everything, there's special-ization. If I want to fix the plumbing in my house, I call a plumber. If I want my oil changed, I take my car to Lube-O-Rama. If I need to go to a doctor, my best bet is to see a specialist for the body part that's giving me problems. I trust the specialists because I'm convinced that they know what they are doing and I'm certain I don't (especially when it comes to anything mechanical!).

In many ways, youth ministry has turned into a specialized field. We are specialists. We are students of teenagers, and we have developed an understanding of their needs, wants, and desires. We continue to add to that wealth of knowledge through every interaction, message, road trip, and crisis counseling session we encounter. We've developed the art of understanding teenagers, even helping them, and have taken an essential position of standing in the gap between teenage culture and an adult world that views the emerging generation as creatures from another planet.

It's no wonder that many in the adult world—the senior pastor, the elders, and the parents—rely heavily on us to disciple their kids. After all, they tell us that's what they hired us for and why we get paid the big bucks…or at least an extra crown in heaven. Many parents are genuinely appreciative of the time, effort, and love we pour into their kids, knowing that teenagers need an adult figure in their lives other than their parents.

While it's good to be appreciated, most youth workers quickly come to see that truly discipling all the teenagers in their group is a nearly impossible task.

Do the math. If a youth worker wants to give each teenager just two hours of undi-vided attention each week in addition to the midweek and Sunday morning group activities, at first glance that seems like a good plan. It's not all that much time.

But multiply that two-hour commitment by the 20 or 30 kids in many groups, and you see the practical problem.

Besides, we have each teenager just four hours out of a given week. Where is that teenager the rest of the time? School takes 40 or 50 hours, and time at home rates a double-digit number of hours. Add in time with friends and perhaps work, and it's obvious that the influence of our few hours can get lost in the avalanche of influences.

The question that haunts me as I wear my youth ministry hat is this: "Am I really discipling the teenagers in my youth group?"

Ultimately, discipleship involves two things.

First, discipleship is a response to Jesus' call for people to follow him.

When we follow Jesus, our worldview is shaped by Jesus. And we embrace the cost of following Jesus, inviting the persecution, testing, and growth that God uses to transform us into the likeness of his Son.

Second, discipleship happens through relationships.

God has provided environments in which those discipling relationships occur. The church is one, and family is another.

Deuteronomy 6 reminds us that, ultimately, parents have responsibility for raising children in the ways of the Lord. Parents have the most time and influence in the life of their children.

The church and the family work together in influencing the faith development of a teenager. But what is the church's role…and what is the family's role?

The fact that there's so much diversity in the makeup of families makes roles a complex issue. But as a shepherd, I keep the following in mind:

- I have a high, holy calling to shepherd those who are under my care. Everything I do in ministry must point teenagers in the direction of following Jesus.
- I'm responsible for good preparation, study, and prayer. I must hold high the power of the Word and teach it believing that the whole gospel is truly transforming. When I take time to study, I'm being faithful and responsible in preparing to shepherd others.

I reserve a study day or half-day each week—and I guard it with my life. I read a lot. I mix the classics with trendy Christian best sellers, believing strongly that the past brings clarity to the future.

- I remember that youth leaders and parents are really on the same team. We all want what's best for the teenagers we know and love.

Too often, in my weak moments, I've perpetuated the "specialist" stereotype by assuming that "parents don't know anything," or that parents "get in the way" of my ministry. But instead, I want parents to *share* in my ministry…and it's my job to keep them connected with our ministry plans. Here are some things I do:

- I try to plan well in advance so that parents have a schedule and know what we are doing.
- On all trips, I include parents in the process. We have a commissioning service where parents can pray over their kids and the kids can pray over their parents. For some, that may be the first time they have ever prayed together (a significant moment).
- We have attempted to redeem Mother's Day and Father's Day by honoring parents at our special youth service.

- When I counsel a teenager, a question that I will eventually ask is "What do your parents think?" or "Have you had a chance to talk with your mom/dad?" Part of the solution usually means bringing a parent into the loop.

Third, I try to remember that though we are "youth ministry specialists," our shepherding role will be incomplete if we do not consider the family systems of which our teenagers are a part. The dreaded phone calls of "Fix my child" or "You need this activity or my child is going to end up worshipping the devil" cannot make us defensive. More likely, these are cries for help. Parents feel scared, inadequate, overwhelmed, tired, frustrated, and like they have failed. They love their kids and are looking for help.

As a result…

- I have attempted to find ways to get parents connected with each other so they can talk about being parents of teenagers and realize that some of their experiences and feelings are normal.
- We have taught a section on teenage development to help parents understand "why my child is acting that way."
- I have tried to take every opportunity to listen, care for, and encourage parents. I pray for them often.
- I try to continue to remind them of their role as parents and thank them for letting me play a small part.

The ultimate hope for teenagers following Jesus is in the redeeming work of our triune God. Our call is to cheer on the people whom God calls into this process. And for "youth specialists," we get to witness the wonderfully "special" mystery of seeing teenagers, moms, and dads fall deeply in love with the One who pursues them.

Steve Argue has been involved with youth ministry for over a decade, serving as a youth pastor, a consultant for youth ministries, a writer, a teacher, and a communicator both nationally and internationally. Currently, Steve lives in Grand Rapids, Michigan, and is the co-founder of Intersect—an organization that seeks to anticipate and connect the emerging generation of leaders in the church. Intersect's Web site is www .intersectcommunity.com, and Steve can be reached at steve@intersectcommunity.com or 1-877-888-5928.

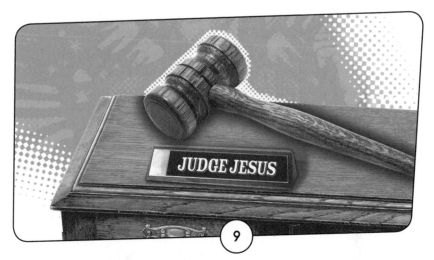

(9)

HANDLING CONFLICT

One of the best ways you can help families deal with conflict is to refer them to other people who can offer more effective assistance than you can. All families face conflict, and many youth workers are equipped to help mediate conflicts. But sometimes those conflicts become more severe and require professional intervention. Even for the everyday conflicts between parents and teenagers, many families can benefit from strategies a professional counselor can share with them.

In anticipation of these needs, create a list of counselors, crisis intervention specialists, family resource centers, and other resources in your area. You may have Christian counselors in your church who can help you compile the information.

Once you have your list, distribute it to parents. Then refer families to those resources as needed. You'll be glad you have the information at your fingertips so you can confidently refer families to professional help.

And be sure to keep your list up to date!

MEDIATION BOARD

When corporations disagree and face possible lawsuits, they sometimes look to professional mediators to help them solve their conflicts. Mediators act as neutral third parties who coach others through the process of solving their conflicts themselves so they don't have to end up in court.

If mediation can work for giant corporations arguing over millions of dollars, maybe it can work for the families in your church.

Try this idea: Create a mediation board made up of a small group of volunteer parents and students. Ask a local Christian counselor to train them in techniques to mediate conflicts. Then make the families in your church aware of this resource. Let them know they can use this mediation board to help family members solve conflicts. Also make sure they know that the board includes both teenagers and parents—so the group is fair and impartial. Then allow this group to mediate conflicts between parents and youth (or other family members) as requested.

One special note: Make sure this is a small team that will maintain confidentiality and that will not be intimidating to families in your church. Families will need to know they can trust this board to be accepting and not to share with others about their struggles.

LOOK AROUND

Sometimes conflicts between youth and their parents just arise and must be dealt with when and where they happen. However, at other times, parents know that they must talk to their youth about an issue that is likely to lead to some type of conflict or confrontation. Offer them some advice about choosing the context for conflict to help make these times as successful as possible.

- **Look around!** Encourage parents to choose a place for discussion that is "neutral" turf or their kids' turf. Calling the youth into the parents' room or having them sit across from dad's office desk does not usually present an atmosphere of discussion (both scream "lecture"). Try to discuss the issue in a family area of the house or in the youth's room.

- **Watch the time!** Youth seem to love staying up late, but these late hours usually are not good for facing up to difficult situations. Even if the youth does not appear tired, he or she has probably already had enough conflict and difficulties for one day. At the same time, parents are usually too tired to think and talk rationally about any subject when bedtime is only a few minutes away.

- **Think about the big picture!** The night of the prom. The night before the SATs. The night after losing a championship game. These usually are bad times for conflict. If possible (admitting that some issues must be dealt with immediately), parents should be encouraged to think about the other events going on in their kids' lives when choosing a time to confront a difficult issue.

Be sure to offer parents input and support so they will have the courage to face some of these difficult situations. The more willing and able they are in managing conflict, the more successful they will be as parents.

JUDGE JESUS

Question: Are there ever conflicts in youth groups?

Answer: Yes.

Question: Are youth groups prepared to handle conflict?

Answer: They can be.

Most conflict resolution in the real world takes place before a judge or a mediator. The court-room model is also seen in several places in the Bible. The

presiding judge and mediator in the biblical model is Jesus. Here is a creative process for taking group conflicts before Judge Jesus.

This idea courts the service of three youth mediators. To assist the disagreeing parties, a fellow youth will be appointed as an advocate for each party in the conflict. All parties will base their arguments and decisions on the premise of what Jesus would do. The following are guidelines for your youth court:

- What would Jesus do? This must be the guiding question for every argument and any decision issued by the mediators.
- Three youth mediators—Before they can issue a decision, at least two mediators have to agree. This group should be selected at the beginning of the year before a conflict arises so they are seen as impartial. Have two or three alternates in case the conflict involves one of your mediators.
- Youth advocates—There should be one for each party. Let the parties choose their own advocates from the group. The advocate presents the client's case to the mediators in written and oral form. The advocates and their parties are allowed to address only the mediators and not each other at the hearing.
- Bailiff—This should be the youth leader or another adult respected by the group. The bailiff should keep order in a kind and respectful manner.

- Nonbinding decision—The court's decision should be nonbinding.
- Consent—All parties should give their consent for having the conflict heard by the youth court.
- Private/public hearing—Encourage the conflicting parties to have the hearing take place in front of the entire group. If anyone is not comfortable with a public forum, hold the hearing in private.

While there is no guarantee that this will truly resolve the conflict, it is certain that the process will lead everyone to the feet of Judge Jesus. Your youth will come away with a deeper perspective of how God judges us. They will also realize that their Christian principles can be applied to real life. Thank you, Judge Jesus!

WATERLOO OR GETTYSBURG: PICK YOUR BATTLES

Not all things are worth fighting about. If a parent's relationship with his or her teenager seems volatile at times, this is especially important. Have parents think for a moment about what sorts of issues they and their teenagers fight (or argue) about. Some of them may include the following:
- Amount of time spent on the phone, cell phone, or Internet
- Styles of clothes, hair, makeup, body piercing, tattoos, and so on
- Friends and boy/girlfriends
- Curfew
- Choice of music, movies, television programs, magazines, and radio stations
- Amount of time spent with family, doing homework, applying to college, and working

Now have parents determine *why* they fight about these things. For instance, did they argue about curfew last week because their teenagers wanted to be out later than usual *or* because their teenagers were with people they consider a negative influence?

In making "rules" for teenagers, parents should remember the difference between *virtue* and *rule keeping.* Have them consider their household rules. Do they help instill virtuous character in their teenagers? Rather than operating with a rigid set of rules, parents should determine to help their teenagers learn lessons of choices and consequences (even good choices have consequences—they're just good ones!) and what it means to have a virtuous character.

So rather than saying, "You can't wear that!" parents should encourage their teenagers to dress modestly in ways that reflect their bodies as the image of God. Rather than setting a permanent 10:30 curfew for Saturday nights, parents might allow flexibility depending upon where their teenagers are and whom they are with. If they do stay out late, parents might allow them to experience the consequence of their choice by still having to attend the 8:30 a.m. worship service at church!

To learn more about parent-teenager relationships (and much more!), encourage parents to read *The Family: A Christian Perspective on the Contemporary Home* by Jack O. Balswick and Judith K. Balswick (Baker).

TWO SIDES TO EACH STORY

When conflict ensues (between parents and youth, you and youth, you and parents, and youth themselves) have both parties involved write out their stories. Be sure to distinguish between *fact* and *feeling*. A *fact* is what happened. A *feeling* is an emotional response. So to say, "She made me feel worthless!" is a fuzzy combination of the two. Rather, distinguish between what happened and how it was responded to: "She said my worship leading sounded like a frog on helium and then I felt worthless."

Encourage both parties to write out their sides of the story on one page each. Make sure they distinguish between fact and feeling! Once they've finished, have each read his or her story to the other (the other party *may not interrupt* while the story is being read). Once both stories are read, discuss what happened. Pray. Talk about how it's OK for people to disagree and be angry, but as followers of Christ, we are called to show mercy to one another.

MOUTH TO MOUTH

Out the window of the youth group room, Youth Pastor Sally sees Single Volunteer Alex offer a ride home to 16-year-old Youth Group Member Sarah after a church event. He gives her a big hug, and they get into the car together. Sally is troubled by this; the rule is that volunteers are never to be alone with youth group members of the opposite sex. She wonders if something inappropriate is going on and asks other volunteers if they have noticed anything. Soon everyone's buzzing and whispering. That is, except Alex, who has no idea what is being said, no opportunity to defend himself or admit he has overstepped a boundary.

We've all seen it happen. One person is angered by or "concerned about" the actions of another and tells everyone but that person. Soon everyone is talking about and perhaps exaggerating the conflict—everyone except the people who are directly involved, the ones who should be discussing it! This kind of talk can be especially poisonous to churches; it can blow quickly out of proportion and lead to long-term disagreements and misunderstandings. One way to avoid this unhealthy cycle is to make it a point never to triangulate.

If you have a conflict with a parent or adult volunteer, speak directly with him or her first if possible and resist the temptation to discuss the problem with a third party. If you must seek advice on a particularly troubling situation involving a youth, parent, or volunteer, ask your senior pastor, a trusted friend or adviser who is not involved in the situation, or your spouse, rather than another volunteer or parent. In the same way, discourage triangulation among your staff. Make it clear to them that if they disagree with something you have done, you expect them to come to you first and you will do the same.

TAKE THE INITIATIVE

If there is conflict between you and a parent, be the one to take the initiative to try and resolve it. Invite the parent out for coffee in a nonthreatening, neutral setting. Often having the chance to relate to the youth leader face to face will do a lot to defuse the situation. Then discuss the issue that's causing conflict, following these stages. It might be a good idea to talk the parent through this outline so he or she knows where the conversation is headed.

- Listen to each other's perspective. Let one person talk at a time and the other listen without interrupting or defending himself or herself. Try to understand why the parent feels the way he or she does; the parent will do the same for you.
- Find common ground. What areas can you agree on? Perhaps that you both want young people to grow in their relationship with God.
- List possible solutions without judging them at this stage. Try to think of solutions from which you both can benefit—think win-win.
- Evaluate the solutions you have thought of. This is where you may need to agree to disagree on some aspects.
- Reach an agreement together. This may take negotiation and patience.

If it's impossible to reach an agreement, at least you will have shown that you can be responsible in addressing the issue. You may need to then refer the matter to your supervisor or church leaders. Perhaps the next step would be to arrange a meeting between the parent, your church leader, and yourself.

AN EYE FOR AN EYE?

Revenge is natural, or at least that's what the movies try to tell us. If someone hurts you, then you need to hurt that person back. But that's not what Jesus taught. In the Sermon on the Mount, he said we should turn the other cheek and love our enemies instead of trying to get back at them (Matthew 5:38-48).

If a parent has been critical of the way you do youth work or there has been some conflict between you, it's very easy to feel defensive and to want to avoid that parent in the future. But don't. Find a topic that the parent knows a lot about, and ask his or her advice. Invite the parent to come and participate as a volunteer in a youth session. Think of some way you need his or her help, and then ask for it. Make a point of greeting the parent whenever you see him or her, making eye contact and offering a handshake. Thank that parent for any support he or she does give you in the youth work. Be the one who makes peace, and you will be blessed.

WHO'S IN THE DRIVER'S SEAT?
BY MARK DEVRIES

"That which goes deepest to the heart goes widest to the world."
—Earl Palmer

I was less than thrilled when Craig, a father of a new seventh grader, announced in September that he would be driving for our junior high ski trip. As I would soon learn, Craig was used to being in the driver's seat.

He owned his own business, spent a good bit of time on the golf course, and had a way of making life work by the sheer force of his personality.

The afternoon of that fateful trip, Craig's colorful-language greeting was enough to deepen my anxiety. And as I stepped across the church parking lot, Craig's wife smiled sheepishly from inside her car and said, "I'll *really* be praying for you."

And so began one of the most challenging trips of my 25 years in youth ministry. Craig spent the entire day not on the slopes but in the emergency room. Oh, it wasn't *his* body that had taken the beating, but the icy Indiana slopes (don't ask) had left their mark on the bones of two of our group. And by the end of the trip, more than a few of us had experienced multiple and profound visits from the vomit fairy.

But in spite of our medical challenges, we managed to pull off three sessions, complete with hilarious stories, music, and on that last morning, a challenge for our kids each to take steps toward following Jesus more faithfully. We prayed hopefully for the Holy Spirit to be busy with our kids, but none of us could have imagined or predicted what God would do with the seemingly disinterested driving dad in the back of the room.

The morning after the trip, I got the call. Not used to doing a lot of waiting, Craig said he had to talk to me, *as soon as possible.* "Something has happened," he said.

When we met for coffee that morning, he was visibly agitated. "It's so weird," he kept saying over and over. "It's so weird."

"It's like something has happened to me, like…" He went on to try to explain what he couldn't explain, that God, over the weekend, in and around a motley group of puking teenagers, had captured his heart. The change was so obvious, so immediate, that I could hear it in his joyful wife's message, "What did you do to my husband?!"

It wasn't long before Craig and Sherri became our most faithful and enthusiastic youth ministry volunteers, teaching their first daughter's class until she graduated from high school. Sherri has cooked and served literally thousands of meals for kids in their home. Craig was the first one with our kids at the sudden death of one of their friends. And now, every year, the two of them personally visit 100 or so college students on their campuses, encouraging them to grow in their love for Jesus.

A few years back, something even stranger happened. Craig closed up his golf shop and joined the staff of our church as our college director. And just a few months from now, that seventh grade little girl will graduate from college, where she and her younger sister are both active in Christian ministries on their campus. Weird.

Over the years I've witnessed firsthand the ripple effects of seeking to engage every parent of every youth in our group. It is amazing how often, in the very act of serving kids, something happens to the *parents*. And when God captures the hearts of parents, their kids' lives are almost always impacted for Christ.

Sounds like youth ministry to me.

Mark DeVries is the author of Family-Based Youth Ministry *(Inter Varsity Press), is founder of Youth Ministry Architects (www.YMArchitects.com), and has served as a youth pastor at First Presbyterian Church in Nashville, Tennessee, for almost 20 years.*

SPIRITUAL SUPPORT FOR PARENTS

PARENT PRAYER PARTNERS

Prayer is a cornerstone for all effective ministry. To mobilize your group's parents to pray, host a parent meeting on the topic. Ask each parent to bring a candle to the meeting.

Gather various craft supplies parents can use to decorate the candles: glue, glitter, permanent markers, lace and ribbon, pins, pipe cleaners, fabric, construction paper, and so on.

During the parents meeting, share how prayer is an essential part of youth ministry and how a network of prayer partners would uplift, encourage, and provide support to the youth staff and the students.

Have parents decorate their candles in a thematic way. Have them pick out a "fruit of the Spirit" found in Galatians 5:22 that they hope to see their students experience through growing into a greater faith in Christ. Then give them time to decorate their candles to reflect their hopes.

Have parents exchange their candles with one another and share the significance of the themes they chose. Encourage each pair to take a few minutes to pray for each other's kids. Have parents swap phone numbers and commit to call each other once a week for prayer requests and praises. The candles can serve as reminders to pray for each other.

Have parents bring their candles to the next meeting and continue swapping them and changing prayer partners.

E-MAIL TIPS

Remember that the most important influence on a person's faith is his or her parents. In ministry to youth, it's worthwhile to spend a little time ministering directly to parents and nurturing their faith. After all, it's the most significant and lasting way you can make a difference in teenagers' lives.

In that spirit, accumulate e-mail addresses for as many of your students' parents as you can. Send a weekly e-mail to parents, including a Scripture selection, a brief meditation, and a parenting tip. You can find parenting tips in books on parenting, on Web sites, from your own experience (if you're a parent), and even among the youth group members. It's a good idea to ask the parents for topic ideas too.

Encourage parents to submit to you their own meditations and tips. Include these in the e-mails you send so parents can encourage each other as well. Be sure to credit your sources; the advice from parents in your group will probably carry more credibility than anything else your e-mails include. Encourage parents to follow up with each other and pray for each other.

FREE COUNSELING

Sometimes parents may wish they could address their personal questions to a professional counselor but feel like they can't get their family involved in counseling. This is a chance to bring the counseling to them.

Hire a professional Christian counselor to come in and give a series of classes on how to survive parenting teenagers. Tell the counselor you are specifically concerned about teaching parents to nurture themselves while caring for their children. Identify for the counselor in advance the issues you know parents are facing, and ask the counselor to address those topics. Make sure there is ample time allowed for question and answer because that may be the heart of how parents will benefit from the class.

Some parents may be concerned about being identified by their family's struggles, so rather than titling the class "Troubled Teenagers," think of a title such as "Q and A on Parenting Teenagers." It's also a good idea to schedule the class during a regular meeting time, such as during a Sunday school hour or as an alternative class during a weekly adult education time.

Tip: Parents are usually more comfortable taking advice from people who have had teenagers of their own.

FAMILY PHOTOS

At an activity that parents and teenagers attend together, take a picture of each family group. If you are likely to be too busy organizing things, assign one of your team to be the photographer. When you get the photos developed, or you print them out, write the names of the parents and teenagers on the back of each picture. Once a week, set aside a regular time to pray for these parents by name, using the photos as a prompt. Pray for any needs that you know about, or pray a simple blessing for them using one of these verses:

"I pray that out of his glorious riches he may strengthen you with power through his Spirit in your inner being, so that Christ may dwell in your hearts through faith. And I pray that you, being rooted and established in love, may have power, together with all the saints, to grasp how wide and long and high and deep is the love of Christ, and to know this love that surpasses knowledge—that you may be filled to the measure of all the fullness of God" (Ephesians 3:16-19).

"The Lord bless you and keep you; the Lord make his face shine upon you and be gracious to you; the Lord turn his face toward you and give you peace" (Numbers 6:24-26).

"May God himself, the God of peace, sanctify you through and through. May your whole spirit, soul and body be kept blameless at the coming of our Lord Jesus Christ" (1 Thessalonians 5:23).

You may not be able to get through all the families every week, so keep the photos in order and rotate through the pile, praying for a few each time. You could give a copy of the photo to each family, with a note on the back to say that you are praying for them.

ELECTRONIC DEVOTIONS

Students can provide spiritual support to their parents and youth sponsors by exercising their cyber-prowess. Get the e-mail addresses of your youth's parents and youth sponsors. Ask student volunteers to sign up on a weekly rotation schedule to write e-mail devotions and send them to the parents and youth sponsors.

Youth will grow as they study God's Word while preparing the devotions. Parents and youth sponsors will be blessed and encouraged.

FAMILIES OF THE WEEK

A youth ministry in the Midwest does something so simple you might think it's hardly noticed by the families of teenagers.

You'd be wrong.

Here's what happens: Each week the family of a teenager in the ministry receives a letter from the youth pastor. The letter announces that the family will be prayed for by the youth ministry staff in the coming week, first at a staff meeting and then by individual volunteers who work in the ministry.

The youth pastor asks if there are any specific prayer requests, and if there are, the family is encouraged to let the youth pastor know. If there aren't specifics, that's OK. The family will still be lifted up in prayer throughout the coming week anyway.

In addition to the power of prayer, there's another power unleashed through this weekly initiative: *the power of being recognized.* Suddenly the youth pastor isn't some distant, slightly odd individual who lives in an alternate reality. Rather, the youth pastor (and entire youth ministry) is someone who cares, who sees the parents, and who supports families.

How do you want to be viewed by parents? As a fun person who never quite outgrew water parks...or as a pastor?

TELE-TALKERS

Here's a great, nonthreatening way to involve students in prayer and thanksgiving for their parents, adapted from Thom and Joani Schultz's book *Creative Faith Ah-Ha's!* (Group Publishing, Inc.). It all begins with a fleet of phones and a church directory.

Let parents know ahead of time that they may be receiving phone calls to find out what they're thankful for this year. Tell them their responses will be incorporated into a worship service presented by the youth group.

Divide up the parents' names and numbers among the teenagers on the calling team. Tell kids they'll be "tele-thankers," hunting for everything people are thankful for. It is better if teenagers don't call their own parents.

Write out a script so students sound legitimate and professional. Say something like "Hi! I'm _____, calling from _____. We're collecting thank you thoughts from our church members to use as prayers in our worship service. We'd like to know what you're most thankful for this year." Have kids jot down the answers they receive, and remind them to thank people for talking to them!

Have another team of students input the thankful comments into a computer for use in worship. Decide if you want to attribute names to specific thanksgivings or present the prayers anonymously. Connecting names with thanks helps build a familylike feeling in your church.

Use the list of responses for a prayer during an upcoming worship service. (You don't need to save this for Thanksgiving; any time will work.) You could set up a computer to scroll the names and prayers on a screen, or you might want to type up the list and distribute it as a handout.

(Adapted from Group Magazine, March/April 2004)

OUTREACH: CROSS MESSAGES

Carry a message of faith and support to parents in need with a special gift—a cross that's been blessed by youth group members' prayers.

First of all, you'll need a supply of simple crosses with chains or necklaces (yarn or leather is fine). If possible, find a church member who can carve small, wooden crosses for you. Then the idea is to identify a parent in need—it could be someone who's been hospitalized or who's in a crisis situation.

At your meeting, have everyone form a circle, and while you hold the cross, offer a prayer for the parent in need. Then pass the cross around the circle. As people each receive the cross, have them tell about a time God helped them through a difficult situation. (How much is shared will differ with each person.) Also have people each think of one particular blessing God gave them during that time (for example, hope, strength, or peace), and ask God to be present in the same way to the person being prayed for.

Soon afterward, representatives from the group should present this cross to the parent in need and explain the prayer process. Not only do young people reach out to those in need, but they also discover the many ways God has been faithful to those in the youth group.

(Adapted from Group Magazine, May/June 2003)

TEACHING TEENAGERS "THE 1 THING"
BY THOM AND JOANI SCHULTZ

We had just finished listening to an energetic naturalist explain the mysteries and wonders of Alaskan wildlife, specifically killer whales. We oohed and aahed over these enormous black and white giants of the sea. We watched as Momma Orca lovingly kept her heavyweight "baby" by her side, all the while teaching the intricacies of swimming and hunting for fish that would guarantee a safer, longer life. And she barely said a word. Her baby was learning by watching and doing—with Mom close by.

We wondered, are we human parents of a teenager all that different from the orcas when it comes to teaching our kids the most important lessons in life? Maybe we can learn a thing or two from nature. For you see, it's modeling what to do and what not to do that promises kids a safer, more secure life now and for eternity.

So if we teach kids by modeling, what exactly are we supposed to teach them? When Jesus spoke to Martha in Luke 10:41-42, he said, "Martha, Martha…you are worried and upset about many things [boy, parents of teenagers can relate to that!], but *only one thing is needed.*" As we've studied that story and its context, we believe the "one thing" Jesus is talking about is a growing relationship with him. But how do we teach teenagers what that growing friendship with Jesus looks and sounds like today in real life?

Unlike orcas, our charge goes beyond modeling swimming and fishing techniques to ensure life. Instinctively (like the orcas?), we as parents have known that we're "on" 24/7—from the day Matt was born. We also know parents are the No. 1 influencer in a child's faith life—for the good or for the bad.

We don't have a choice.

But we do have a choice when it comes to making The 1 Thing paramount. We believe the most important task for us as parents is to bring our son, Matt, closer to his Best Friend, Jesus. We'd like to share three specific ways we've hoped to show our son The 1 Thing:

Use the Power of Eavesdropping

Yes, we believe it's important to talk directly about God to your teenager. But we've found it's also important to talk with others about God—while your teenager is listening in. Allow kids to spy on you. (They do anyway!) Their antennae are up all the time, tuning in to what you say, how you react, and how you make decisions. Lectures don't work. Modeling does.

We know Matt's ears are like a metal detector honing in on a treasure. For example, if the two of us are talking about our day's frustration about a delayed project at work, Matt might overhear us asking each other what God is trying to teach us about patience. Or when a friend is struggling with health issues, he'd hear our desperation and how that friend needs our prayers. We hope he watches where faithful people go first—to The 1 Thing.

Another hint about eavesdropping: If we really wanted to make sure Matt was listening, we'd start talking in hushed voices. It's amazing how closely kids listen if they think you're trying to be discreet. Hey, it works every time!

Use Spontaneous Teachable Moments

Even when going to church wasn't tops on his list, Matt reminded us, "You took me to church even when I didn't want to go. Even when I tried to delay, it just made us late. But we still went." Those tense trips to church offered great teachable moments. We used them to teach the habit and importance of putting God first by attending worship.

OK, that's a churchy example.

But we're also saying teachable moments happen spontaneously, all the time. Watching TV. Hanging out with questionable friends. Dealing with a tough teacher. Using the computer. Honoring commitments. Listening to music. Spending money. Choosing movies. Choosing friends. Winning. Losing. Feeling gratitude and disappointment. Coming home on time. Reading and watching the news. (I think we especially like movies and TV shows because they're like the leaky faucet of teachable moments. There's a steady drip of sex, money, drugs, violence, fame, looks, cheating, information, relationships, and more.)

So what's so cool about a teachable moment?

It's relevant. It's cheap. It's priceless. You don't have to wait for costly curriculum or the perfect moment. Just be on high alert to what's happening around you and your teenager. *Everything* around you is relevant and can merit a God conversation. So be willing to bring up faith talk—not at planned formal times but spontaneously.

Thankfully, God offers families a hefty supply of opportunities to point toward The 1 Thing. For example, when we hear someone cursing, we'll say, "Our family doesn't talk that way. That's because using language like that hurts others and mocks God's name. We love God, and we don't talk about our friends that way." Or when great plans fall through or things don't go our way, these teachable moments prompt us to ask, "Well, God, how are you going to use this? What can we learn from this?"

Or the toughest, most powerful teachable moments are when we as parents blow it. We've both had times when we've lost patience and blown up at Matt. High alert warning: We have to see our shortcomings as teachable moments too. There's nothing more powerful for Matt to hear from one of us than "I'm sorry. I was wrong."

Use Predictable Traditions

Spontaneous teachable moments capture on-the-spot training times. But predictable traditions build consistency, and consistency builds trust. Just imagine: Our own consistency as parents can help communicate God's consistency.

We laugh about our silly family "traditions," but we believe they're another anchor for Matt when it comes to The 1 Thing.

- We eat breakfast together as a family almost every day.
- We pray at meal times and hold hands.
- Mom says, "Morning hug!" which signals a time to hug Mom and Dad.
- We ask, "How was your day?" and we expect elaboration. One-syllable words aren't allowed.
- We pray for each other.
- We celebrate each other's birthdays and our family members' birthdays.
- We and another family celebrate birthdays together; whoever has the birthday gets to choose the dinner spot. (Ask about the time Matt chose the Waffle House!)
- We say goodbye in the mornings with "Love ya, Matt!" (And he replies, "I love you too!")
- We say goodnight in the evenings with " 'Night, Matt. Love ya!"

There are probably more traditions, but you get the idea.

We learned something else about orcas. They may be the most social mammals known to science, and their family bonds are rarely broken. Each orca family uses its own "language," which they never forget—even after being separated from their families for long periods of time.

We pray that long after Matt moves out and starts a family of his own, he will use our "language" of living the everyday, common things that point toward The 1 Thing, a growing relationship with Jesus. Maybe he gave us a hint when he said, "I know Jesus is important 'cause my parents love him. They tell me God loves me. I know God loves me and I love him—and no matter what happens, my mom and dad will always love me."

Thom and Joani Schultz are parents, authors, and church leaders. They've designed innovative resources used in thousands of churches worldwide. They're the authors of many books including the best-selling Why Nobody Learns Much of Anything at Church: And How to Fix It, The Dirt on Learning, Creative Faith Ah-Ha's!, The 1 Thing, *and* Friendship First. *And they write regularly for Group Magazine, Children's Ministry Magazine, and Rev. Magazine. Thom is the president of Group Publishing, the innovative ministry organization he founded in 1974. Joani is Group's chief creative officer.*

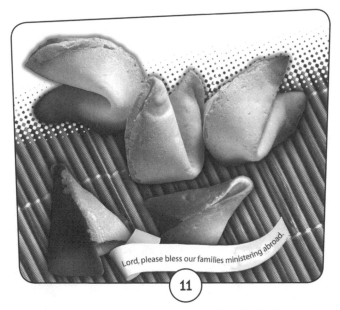

Lord, please bless our families ministering abroad.

11

FAMILY DEVOTION IDEAS

Every family desires to live in harmony and to grow in healthy relationships. To that end, many of your families are ready to share this devotion with one another.

Read 2 Peter 1:3-8. Peter is sharing a radical notion: Our gooodness isn't something we earn. Rather, our goodness comes out of God's divine presence in us.

Many Christians equate their worth and standing to how many good things they do or how many times people affirm them in their lives. Discuss these questions:

- How do parents and children apply this distortion to one another?
- How do our unrealistic expectations of ourselves and of others affect our relationships?
- How do our expectations affect the way we communicate with one another?

Read 2 Peter 1:3-8 again. Remember that goodness comes from Christ's presence in us, and our actions cannot prove us worthy of his love. He has made us worthy by accepting us as we are! Discuss this question:

• Rather than focus on external behavior this week, how can each family member encourage others to grow in their faith?

Some examples may be to say encouraging words, extend forgiveness, pray for your family members, and serve one another before being asked.

Close in prayer, asking God to help you accept yourselves and each other and to welcome Jesus' life-changing power in your lives.

FAMILY TREE

This family devotion will help families learn about and celebrate their heritage—both physical and spiritual.

Before this devotion, do research if necessary to find out names and any other information you can about your family's ancestors.

Find a large piece of poster board. Or if you want to create a keepsake, use canvas or fabric. Work as a family to create a family tree, going back as far as you can. As you work, share as many details as you can regarding the lives and experiences of ancestors. Especially emphasize any details about your spiritual heritage.

When your tree is complete, display it somewhere in your home. Then discuss these questions:

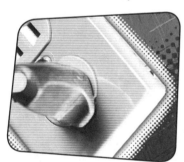

• How did it feel to create this family tree?
• What was it like to learn about our ancestors?
• How do you feel about the people who created our family's heritage?
• What do you especially appreciate about that heritage?
• What do you wish our ancestors had passed along to us?

Read Joshua 24:14-27. Point out that Joshua understood the importance of honoring the spiritual heritage the Israelites had received and passing that heritage along to their descendants. Talk about how you as a family can pass a strong spiritual heritage along to your own descendants.

Close in prayer, thanking God for the legacy you enjoy. Ask God to help your family pass along a strong spiritual heritage to your own descendants.

BEING THE BODY

In this devotion, families will discuss what it means for a family to be part of the body of Christ.

Sit down as a family and talk about what all your family members have in common. Make a list of these characteristics as people mention them.

Then give each person a piece of paper and a pen. Have people write their names at the tops of their papers. Pass the papers around. As each person receives the paper belonging to another family member, have that person write down a few characteristics that make that family member unique. For example, when Cameron receives Emma's paper, Cameron might write, "funny, smart, and caring."

When everyone has had a chance to write on all other family members' papers, give the papers back to their owners. Discuss these questions:

- What was it like to write down characteristics we have in common?
- What was it like to write down these characteristics that make us all unique?
- How does it feel to read the things other family members wrote about you?
- Why do you think God made us all unique and put us in the same family?

Read Romans 12:4-8. Discuss the importance of having various gifts and personalities in a group of Christians who work together to be like Jesus. Talk about the ways your family is part of the body of Christ and how you can work together, using your unique and common characteristics, to minister to others.

Close in prayer, thanking God for what you have in common and asking for grace to celebrate what makes each person unique. Ask God to give you opportunities to work together as a part of the body of Christ.

ON THE TIP OF MY TONGUE

Memorization. The word often brings painful images of spelling words, math formulas, and historical facts. When applied to the Bible, some think of rote memorization of words rattled off without meaning or understanding. However, Scripture memorization does not need to be painful or rote. And memorization is a key (but too often missing) element to strengthening our faith and helping us avoid sin. In Psalm 119:11, the author declares that he has "hidden" God's Word in his heart. Why? So that he "might not sin against" God.

The fact of the matter is that most parents do not memorize Scripture any more than their kids do. As a youth minister, you can encourage Scripture memorization within families by sharing with parents and youth the following ideas:

- Pick a section of the Bible to memorize. Don't grab a random verse, but rather pick verses together that teach an important concept or give a particular encouragement. John 14:1-6 and Colossians 1:15-23 are a couple of examples.

- Set goals. Try to memorize certain sections in a set amount of time.
- Work together. Car rides, family devotions, and morning breakfasts are all times several family members can work on the memorization together.
- Memorize with meaning. Say the verses with meaning and expression even as you practice them together. This will help you think about the verses' meaning *and* will help the verses stick in your head.
- Reward yourselves. When reaching the memorization goal as a family, go out together as a treat for reaching your goal.
- Review. Be sure to go back to past verses so you don't forget what you have learned.

As a youth minister, you might also help families do this by providing them with sections of Scripture to memorize and then giving families time and encouragement to do so. Then you could plan a celebration gathering of parents and youth where the passage can be recited by all who learned it!

THE FAST TRACK TO FASTING

The Bible discusses but doesn't entirely explain the spiritual discipline of fasting. Here is an idea to send home with your students for a family devotion on the subject.

First discuss what kinds of things distract family members from God and from the important purposes of their lives. To explain fasting, use a plant as an object lesson. A plant grows toward the closest sources of light. If you turn a plant on its side, it can literally grow sideways toward the sun.

People work the same way. We grow toward whatever feeds us. If we find satisfaction in a hundred other things before we look to God, we may never get to the point of growing toward God. Fasting just turns off all of the distracting sources of light in our lives so we can focus on God. Discuss how family members might cut those things out for the next month. Then read Matthew 6:16-18 and discuss the purpose of fasting.

DO A BOOK STUDY!

Many parents may feel like their teenagers are outgrowing family devotions. When that happens, it's time to set aside the "inspirational readings" and do a book study! Give parents these ideas to perk up their family devotions:

- Before you start, hand out Bibles to your family members and take time to browse through them. Watch what sorts of books catch your teenager's eye. Does Levitical law fascinate him? Does she ask lots of questions about Paul's letters? Does apocalyptic literature capture his imagination? Do the differences between the gospels cause her to pause and consider?

- With your family, discuss what sort of book to study—history, law, prophetical literature, poetry, or letters. Once you've narrowed down the genre, determine a specific book. (It may be good to start with a shorter book rather than Psalms, for instance.)
- Take your teenager to a local Christian bookstore. Browse through the study guide section (and maybe even the commentaries, if your teenager is interested). If you can't decide which study guide you want, most Christian bookstores have a generous return policy. (Ask first!) Buy several, discuss them with your small group (or family), and return the ones you decide not to use.

Now it's time to study! In addition to the study guide, you may want to try the following things:

- Read the text by paragraphs rather than by chapters and verses. Sometimes chapters and verses interrupt sentences and paragraphs (and thus the train of thought).
- Try reading the same section in several different translations.
- Read the text according to how it was written. For instance, if it's a letter, have one person read the letter aloud to everyone else. If it's a story, take turns reading different parts. (Select a narrator to read the sections in between the quotes.)
- If you have younger children, include them by allowing them to draw pictures of the paragraphs and listen to the readings.

For a good introduction to studying the Bible, you (and your teenager) may want to read *How to Read the Bible for All Its Worth* (3rd edition) by Gordon D. Fee and Douglas Stuart (Zondervan).

UPS AND DOWNS

This is a good activity for families to do when something comes to an end—for example, at the end of the year, the end of a school term, or the end of the holidays. Send details of this activity inside a Christmas card to the family, or with a program for the next term, and suggest that the family do this activity before the first meeting of the youth group.

The family will need a large sheet of paper with "Ups" written on one side and "Downs" on the other side. Put the paper on the table with the word "Downs" showing, and get everyone to sit around it, each with a pen. Then invite everyone to think back over the last year, the last term, or the holidays. What have been the down moments for them—the things that went wrong or made them sad?

Let everyone write for a few minutes and then start to talk about what they have written. Take time to listen if people are upset. When everyone has finished writing, invite each person to say a short prayer offering these downs to God. Then turn the page over and do the same with the ups—first letting people write, then talk, and then pray. Read together Isaiah 43:1-3. Finish by thanking God that he has been with them through the ups and downs.

WHEN I WAS YOUR AGE...

Write 1 Timothy 4:12 on index cards, one for each member of your group: "Don't let anyone look down on you because you are young, but set an example for the believers in speech, in life, in love, in faith and in purity." Write these bulleted items below:

- What was your faith like when you were my age? How did you become a Christian?
- What helped you grow as a Christian?
- Talk together about whether you are setting a good example in these areas.

Invite young people to take these cards home with them and talk about them with their parents. Get them to ask one or both of their parents to find photos of themselves when they were the same age as their sons and daughters are now. Suggest that they make a cup of coffee for their mom or dad and create some space where they won't be interrupted. Then, together, they should talk through the items on the card. This will give parents a chance to explain how and when they came to faith and what has helped their faith develop.

GOOD FORTUNE COOKIES

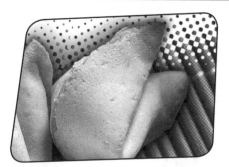

Help families plan a missions-centered devotion by encouraging a Chinese takeout night. After enjoying a Chinese meal, family members should discuss the important work done by missionaries abroad.

Challenge families to share Bible verses that serve as the basis of the work missionaries do and pray together for those serving so selflessly abroad.

Use tiny slips of paper (like those inside fortune cookies) to write prayers for blessings and good fortunes for families ministering to others in foreign countries, especially those closed to the gospel.

You may provide information about specific missions that your church supports to help families pray intelligently about real needs.

DEVOTIONS WITH ZING

Devotions are important for family spiritual growth, but it's easy to fall into a rut. Have families try these ideas to hold their teenagers' interest and liven up their family devotion time:

- Have parents leave devotion-related, pun-inspired notes around the house as clues. For example, they could highlight every letter I and number 4 in the note and then center their devotion on Matthew 5:38-39 ("eye for eye").
- Suggest that parents include music—but let their teenagers pick the songs and crank them up!
- Parents could reserve a family-favorite snack or dessert for devotion time only.
- Have parents start with a joke-telling time, allowing the corniest joke teller to win a prize.
- Parents could have everyone use a commercial jingle to express the moral of the devotion.
- Suggest that parents hold their devotions in novel locations: in the attic, in a tent, while tailgating at an ice cream parlor, on the doghouse roof, or in a tree.
- Tell parents that they could use walkie-talkies to conduct their devotion during "lights out."

(Adapted from Group Magazine, May/June 2004)

PRAYER TRIPS

Have your youth's family prayer times become routine, uneventful—or nonexistent? Perhaps they need a change of scene. Suggest these prayer trips for a new devotion experience:

- Discount store—Ask each family member to find an item under $2 that represents one of God's graces. Offer prayers of praise to God for each item, thanking him for showing his grace in everyday ways. Place the items on your dining room table, and have everyone repeat their prayers when your family says grace.

- Parking garage—Have each family member lead the family in a search for a car with the fish symbol on it. Have that family member pray for the car owner's protection and for unity in God's kingdom.
- Amusement park—While you're waiting in line for a ride or game, encourage family members to pray silently for each person they make eye contact with.
- Sporting event—Have your family sit quietly and listen to God for the first five minutes of a game. Take a few minutes to pray as a family, asking God to help you listen to his commands, even during "noisy" times.

(Adapted from Group Magazine, July/August 2002)

EASTER DEVOTIONS

Help parents focus their family's attention on Easter truths with these ideas:
- Rent and watch the video *Jesus of Nazareth*. Then discuss these questions: Was the depiction of Christ and his life accurate? What were you thinking and feeling during the Crucifixion and Resurrection scenes? What would you have left out of the video? added?
- Wash each other's feet. Read aloud John 13:1-17 and discuss these questions: How did it feel to wash each other's feet? Why did Jesus give us this example to follow? What was Jesus showing us by doing this? How can we "wash others' feet"?
- Plan and prepare a traditional Passover or Seder meal. Check out a book from your local library on the Passover or Seder meal to act as a guide. After the meal, read aloud Exodus 12:1-30 and Mark 14:12-26. Discuss these questions: How does the Jewish Passover meal compare with the Lord's Supper? Then read aloud John 1:29-34; I Corinthians 5:6-8; and 1 Peter 1:13-21. Discuss: Compare the lamb in the Exodus verses and the Lamb of God in the New Testament verses.

(Adapted from Group Magazine, March/April 2000)

WISE MEN STILL SEEK HIM

In the church, January 6 is traditionally recognized as Epiphany—the day the wise men visited Jesus in Bethlehem.

Epiphany means "disclosure" or "unveiling," and in the history of the church, it refers to various occasions when Jesus was revealed to people: his birth, the Magi's visit, his baptism, the wedding at Cana, and his awaited second coming. Encourage families to remember this special post-Christmas holiday with these ideas:

- Read aloud Matthew 2:1-12. Ask: Why did the wise men say they had come to see Jesus? Why did they—and why do we—worship him? The wise men actually saw Jesus in the flesh; how do we seek him today? What does Jesus' "unveiling" teach us about God?

- Save one Christmas gift for each person to open on January 6. Thank God for revealing his Son to us and sending him as a sacrifice for our sins.
- Following the Magi's example, have family members each think about one thing they could give to Jesus in the coming year; for example, they can volunteer at church or spend special time with him in prayer each day. Have family members write down their ideas, then wrap these "gifts" and put them under the tree on January 6. After the Christmas season, display these presents in a prominent place in your home as a reminder of what family members have promised.

(Adapted from Group Magazine, January/February 2000)

FAST COMPANY

Challenge adult leaders and students in your youth group to a once-a-month fast.

Invite participants to skip breakfast, lunch, and snacks throughout the day. That evening, have the family gather for a Prayer, Praise, and Pizza event.

The small sacrifice of giving up food, even briefly, will add greatly to this time of worship and prayer. Be sure to have families pray specifically for God's blessing and direction for the youth ministry. Hold a debriefing about the fast at your next youth group meeting.

(Adapted from Group Magazine, March/April 2003)

FAMILY: THE MOST POWERFUL FORCE IN A YOUNG PERSON'S LIFE
BY JIM BURNS

The most powerful force in a young person's life is his or her family. Long before they entered your youth group and long after they leave the group, your kids will be greatly impacted by their families for good *and* for bad. I don't think we in youth ministry have done an effective enough job of integrating the faith of our students with their family lives.

When I first was involved in youth ministry, I loved and appreciated many of the moms and dads. They were incredible people, but it never dawned on me that part of my job as a youth worker was to facilitate helping the families of the kids in my youth group succeed. Never once did I proactively make a decision to serve the needs of their families or give their parents resources to help them build a spiritual legacy in their own families. Thank God, some of the parents took their call from God to nurture their children in the faith seriously. Sure, some of the kids had a good youth group experience, but it could have been even more effective if I had known then what I know now about family-based youth ministry.

A youth worker recently shared this thought with me, and I think she really meant it: "The church's role is to be equippers of families. What we ought to do is let the kids drop their parents off at church, train the parents, and send them back into their mission field, their home, to grow Christians!" I don't know if this would ever happen in the church, but it is not such a bad idea, since the most powerful force (besides God) in a student's life is his or her family. I don't think I truly understood this concept for youth ministry until just recently. Sure, the youth group is incredibly impacting and, frankly, there is often a season in a kid's life when the youth workers are liked and listened to more than the parents. But, nevertheless, in the long haul, it is our families that play a much more important role in shaping who we are and what we do with our lives.

The biblical role model is found in what the majority of Jews say is the most quoted Scripture in the entire Bible. It is found in Deuteronomy 6:4-9 and is quoted every morning and evening in a good Orthodox Jewish home. When Jesus was asked what the greatest commandment was, he immediately quoted part of this Scripture. Here's what it says: "Hear, O Israel: The Lord our God, the Lord is one. Love the Lord your God with all your heart and with all your soul and with all your strength. These commandments that I give you today are to be upon your hearts. Impress them on your children. Talk about them when you sit at home and when you walk along the road, when you lie down and when you get up. Tie them as symbols on your hands and bind them on your foreheads. Write them on the doorframes of your houses and on your gates."

Apparently the biblical role of the parent is to impress faith in a positive way into the lives of his or her children. Unfortunately, most Christian parents don't see it that way or simply don't know what to do. I believe it is time for a "new paradigm" that comes from the Scripture long before youth ministry was ever invented. It is the role of the church to mentor parents and the role of parents to mentor their children, and then the legacy of faith continues to the next generation.

I've gathered some interesting statistics to back up family-based youth ministry:

- Newsweek magazine and the Children's Defense Fund revealed that the following factors were most influential on kids (in order): parents, extended family, coaches, teachers and other adults outside the home, peers, and media.
- According to a study at Abilene Christian University, students who reported having positive family communication were twice as likely to perceive God as important in their lives as those who reported negative family communication.
- Search Institute revealed that nothing influences the faith maturity of teenagers as much as "family religiousness."
- According to a study conducted by George Barna, 78 percent of youth indicated that their parents had more influence on their decision making than anyone else in their lives.

All of us in youth ministry instinctively know that the family plays an important part in the spiritual development of our kids, but few of us have been able to figure out the right program. Well, here is the good news/bad news: *Family-based youth ministry is not a program but rather a mind-set.* Everything we do in youth ministry should be done with that thought in mind. This doesn't mean, as some would suggest, that we re-create youth ministry. No, we just need to include the mind-set of the importance of family in all aspects of our ministry.

How?

I don't think there are easy answers, but I do think there are answers. Start small and ask the question "What am I doing to help the families of my students succeed?" Remember, your task is to support and strengthen the existing family unit. No matter what the family situation is, you can never take the place of the parent.

Here are a few tips:

- **Communicate clearly**—The number one "felt need" in a recent survey of parents who had students involved in youth ministry was "we need communication and information." What are you teaching on? Who are the leaders who are influencing my kids? What are the dates for this coming year's summer camp? The questions are practical and fair.

You can provide the clear communication they need through parent newsletters, information nights, a Web site, fliers, and all the basic ways to communicate. They don't need flash; they want to be in the know.

- **Assist parents**—Most youth workers aren't parents of teenagers (unless you are an old guy like Doug Fields), but you can assist parents to understand the unique world of teenagers. You are probably more of an expert on teenage culture than they are. Even if parents aren't all that active in your church, they typically do care about their kids.

Here are a few ideas: Create seminars for parents on important subjects centering on adolescence (sexuality, understanding the teen culture, building morals and values, energizing your family's spiritual life, helping your child get a college scholarship). Use "an expert" from afar, find an authority in the church, buy a video curriculum program, or start a small group for parents of adolescents.

- **Involve parents**—People support what they help create. I think some of the healthiest youth ministries in the country have parents taking active roles. Not every parent needs to teach, but he or she can do something. Kids need good parental role models. I'm suggesting these days to ask parents for 100 percent involvement in one aspect of the ministry. (You'll never get 100 percent, but it's still worth the ask!)

Parents can be sponsors, volunteer to drive on retreats, supply food, pray, raise funds, lead a small group, be on an advisory board, chaperone events, open up their homes for a meeting, volunteer with office and clerical responsibilities, write and edit the parents newsletter, and the list can go on.

As you attempt to develop a more family-friendly ministry, don't change your entire program; do change your mind-set. Keep it simple and start small. Your family-focused ministry just may be one of the most effective ways for you to invest in building a spiritual legacy for your students.

Jim Burns, Ph.D., is president of HomeWord/YouthBuilders. He is author of the book Partnering With Parents in Youth Ministry: The Practical Guide to Today's Family-Based Youth Ministry *(Regal Book). Two million people listen daily to Jim on the radio and also receive help at HomeWord.com.*

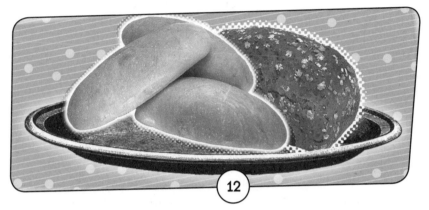

12

MEETINGS WITH PARENTS

ADDRESSING BEHAVIOR PROBLEMS

When you are having trouble with a student's behavior in your group, it's a good idea to meet with that student's parents so they know what's going on and can help you address the problem.

Set up a meeting with both the student and the student's parent(s). This meeting should take place at the church office or in their home. Open the meeting with prayer, then spend some time getting to know the family and talking about positive characteristics you see in the student. Affirm that student's potential to be a valuable and contributing member of your group, and assure the parent that you'd like to keep the student actively involved in your group.

Then lay out your assessment of the problem, and allow everyone an opportunity to agree or disagree. As you talk, continue to be encouraging and affirm the positive. Lay out a strong vision for what the group should be like and why it needs to be safe for everyone—for that student and for everyone else. Then discuss what needs to happen in order for this student to support that vision. Lay out clear expectations and action steps for going forward, including consequences. Then ask the student and the parents to agree that they will pursue this plan of action along with you.

Close the meeting in prayer. Then open yourself up to meeting with the student's parent(s) alone at another time. Parents may have additional questions or input they won't want to share in front of the student.

INFORMAL AFFIRMATION

When it comes to interacting with parents, don't wait for formal meetings or invitations to dinner. And don't fall into the trap of interacting with only the parents of the "stars" in your group—or of the students in your group who need lots of extra attention.

Make it a point to regularly find parents at church or in other settings when their teenagers are around. In front of the teenagers, tell the parents how great their students are—and praise their parenting skills as well. For example, you might say something like "Did Devon tell you how good he's getting at playing the guitar for our group? Thanks for making the effort to drive him to practices. It makes a big difference for everyone." If you catch parents when their teenagers aren't around, go ahead and do this anyway—parents still need to hear positive words about their kids.

Even though these meetings are informal, they may take planning on your part. For some students, you may need to put a lot of thought into finding some positive words to share. For others, you'll need to figure out what their parents look like so you can find them in a crowd! You may even want to keep track of which parents you've talked to lately and which ones you haven't. Go out of your way to talk to the ones who are hard to find. A handshake and a few words from you can make an enormous difference to a discouraged parent!

HOUSE TOUR

Every now and then, invite yourself over to a student's house. You may want to concentrate on the families you don't know that well, especially the ones who aren't very vocal about what they expect from your youth ministry program.

Once you're at the house, ask the student's parent(s) to take you on a tour of the home. During your tour, you can use the various rooms in the home to remind you of questions you can ask the parents. These questions should focus on getting to know the family and their needs. Here are some questions you might ask:

- In a kitchen—Who does most of the cooking in your family? Why?
- In a living/family room—How does your family like to spend an evening at home?
- In a student's bedroom—What would you do with this room if you had an unlimited budget? What would your son/daughter like to do with it?
- In a bathroom—In this family, who spends the most time in front of the mirror?
- In a dining room—Do you eat a lot of meals at home, or do you find yourself eating on the run?

- In a garage—Who does the most driving in your family? Why?
- In a basement—Do you have any special collections or heirlooms your family is proud of?

After the tour, use the information you discovered to continue the conversation about the family. Use this time to get to know what the family wants, expects, and needs from the youth ministry program.

E-Z PARENT MEETING

Parent meetings can sometimes be stressful on a youth leader. Make it easier on yourself by having your youth sponsor the parent meeting. After you have decided on a date, allow the youth group to decide what food to have with the meeting. It could be an ice-cream sundae meeting or a tea and cookies meeting or whatever they choose. The easier the preparation, the better, since students will be doing the setup and cleanup. Then use some youth group time to have your youth create written invitations to their parents. Have them write the correct time and date and decorate the invitations in a way appropriate to the event. Collect and mail the invitations.

Assign students to help buy the food for the parent meeting and to bring it with them on the scheduled night. Some students should arrive early on the night of the parent meeting to prepare the food. As parents arrive, students should greet them and serve them the food and help the parents settle in. After all the parents have food and are settled, you can run the meeting while the youth eat and clean up (an adult volunteer to supervise this process is recommended).

By the time the meeting is over, everyone has snacked and everything is cleaned up. This allows you to focus on the content of the meeting and encourages parents to come because their kids are there anyway, ready to serve them!

FINDING PURPOSE IN STEAL THE BACON

Parents will sometimes get no feedback from their teenagers as to how they like the youth group, other than a brief grunt before they run upstairs to do homework. The default assumption may be that you just play games with the teenagers for an hour or just read the Bible together. Either way, it's time for an introduction.

Schedule a meeting with parents, telling them ahead of time, "I want to explain the purpose of the youth ministry." Remember that in this meeting, you are doing ministry for them as well. Some of them may not even know what churches are for.

As parents enter, give them a survey asking them what they most want from the youth program and offering a list of options of ways to volunteer. The list should offer a variety of options based on level of time commitment (drive to events, host a dinner, help on an overnighter, and so on).

During the meeting, have a well-thought-out, 10-minute explanation of what you would love to accomplish in the life of a teenager before he or she graduates and what programs and activities you are offering to help accomplish that goal. Offer book reviews of three important books for parents to read regarding the lives of teenagers today.

To conclude, allow for a question-and-answer period. Give parents your phone number or e-mail address so they can contact you with further questions. A top-notch youth worker would continue to stay in contact by sending out monthly e-mails to parents, keeping them informed of your activities.

CREATIVE PRACTICAL HOSPITALITY

Part of getting to know people involves going to each other's homes. But sometimes this can involve a lot of work, expense, and cleanup. Some groups of people resort to potluck, with everyone bringing a dish and hoping it will go together. Sometimes it does; sometimes it doesn't. You can do potlucklike things without the madness of potluck! Remember, when a simple solution is chosen, it's a lot easier for youth leaders to have parents over (or vice versa). Utilize the following ideas for having parents to your home for tasty, creative, and simple meals:

Simple Supper

Provide several loaves of hearty bread. Put some virgin olive oil in a shallow dish. Arrange condiments (mayonnaise, mustard, horseradish, pickles, olives) on a tray. Ask parents to bring plates of cheeses, sliced meats, spreads, sliced raw vegetables, and fruit. (It works best to ask specific people to bring specific things.) People can make sandwiches or just eat chunks of bread dipped in oil with pieces of meat and vegetables on the side.

Salad Supper

Mix up a variety of lettuces in a big bowl. (Some ideas include romaine, green/red leaf, iceberg, and endive.) Ask parents to bring chopped hard-boiled eggs, cooked garbanzo beans, tomatoes, slices of meat, grated cheese, sunflower seeds, croutons, and bread. Make a simple vinegar and oil salad dressing.

Waffle or Pancake Meal

Determine if you will make waffles or pancakes (depending on if you own a griddle and/or waffle iron). Mix up several batches of batter (at least one savory and one sweet). Start cooking the waffles or pancakes, and put the cooked ones in the oven to keep warm. Ask parents to bring grated cheese, bacon and/or sausage, syrup, honey, jam or jelly, butter, sour cream or plain yogurt and powdered sugar (a surprisingly great combination!), chopped fruit, and ice cream. Be creative with the waffles or pancakes! You can cook berries, chocolate chips, grated cheese, and spices or herbs into them. (Don't try out something totally new on the parents, though!)

Curry Meal

Make a large batch of chicken or lentil curry (or both, if you have lots of people coming over). Cook a big pot of rice. Have parents bring chopped peanuts, almonds, raisins, shredded carrots, yogurt mixed with cucumber, chopped hot peppers, and chutney. Put rice in a bowl, top with curry sauce, and sprinkle desired additions on top according to taste.

Ice Cream Meal

Provide several gallons of ice cream. Ask parents to bring chopped fruit, nuts, chocolate, caramel, strawberry syrup, cookie crumbs, and granola. Though ice cream meals are not a healthy way to eat weekly, it's fun to eat ice cream as the main course once in a while. (Make sure no parents are diabetic and/or lactose intolerant before planning this meal. They'd feel left out!)

(Adapted from More-With-Less Cookbook *by Doris Janzen Longacre [Herald Press])*

A PROBLEM SHARED...

Arrange a get-together for parents where they can talk about the difficulties they face in their parenting. Tell them that problems will be shared anonymously, that the evening will be about parents helping each other find solutions, and that you will be there to listen and learn. Ask them in advance to give you the questions they want answered or the problems they are trying to deal with at the moment. You could send around a form for them to fill out and return to you anonymously. Type these questions and problems onto slips of paper, and put them in a bowl.

On the evening of the get-together, provide food and drinks to help parents relax. Pass the bowl of questions around. Each parent will pull out a slip, read what's on it, and give a response. The issue can then be discussed, with other people giving their perspectives and what has worked for them. Since the problems and questions are aired anonymously, people will be more likely to be honest in their questions and their responses, although you may also find that people are willing to own up to their particular issues once they see that other people will be supportive. It's very encouraging as parents to hear that other people have the same problems as you. At the end, encourage people to get together again and keep talking to and supporting each other.

A TRIP TO THE MOVIES

Arrange a trip to the movie theater with the parents of the young people in your group. Don't choose anything highbrow or intellectual; choose a film that their kids will be into at the moment or one that has something to say about youth culture. You'll get the chance to socialize with parents and build relationships in a relaxed setting, and you can take the opportunity to discuss with them afterward the themes that come up in the film. Over coffee, find out their reactions to any violence, sexual activity, or swearing in the film. Talk about what their teenagers might find attractive about the film and what they might learn from it. Point out any spiritual issues that came up in the film, and help parents think about how they might discuss these themes with their teenagers.

ROOM INSPECTION

At your next parent–youth sponsor meeting, ask everyone to take a seat on the floor. Give each person a pen and a piece of paper. Challenge people to write down every item in the room in one minute's time. When the minute is up, share what has been written.

Ask them to do the exact same activity again, this time listing things in the room that no one has already observed on the first list. With a minute on the clock, see how many items they can come up with that were overlooked during the first round. Afterward, share aloud.

Do the same activity a third time. Is anyone able to come up with something new? This calls for careful scrutiny—leave no cheese-puff crumb or dust ball unturned! Again, have a time of sharing.

Then have people use this same procedure to make a list (general to specific) of things they have observed about the youth program—not rants, criticisms, or even suggestions but simply observations. Afterward, use the list as a springboard into a discussion about how to improve the youth program together as a team.

SHOW YOU CARE

Care packages during finals week are common for college students. Why not offer the same encouragement to your students while they're in high school?

Hold a meeting with parents in which you help parents put together care packages for their teenagers with small toys for stress relief, along with a selection of late-night snacks, such as candy bars, microwave popcorn, hot cocoa packets, and chewing gum.

Use a desktop publishing program to make stickers or refrigerator magnets with the following verses on them: "I press on toward the goal to win the prize for which God has called me heavenward in Christ Jesus" (Philippians 3:14) and "I can do everything through him who gives me strength" (Philippians 4:13).

Have parents add notes of encouragement that cheer their teenagers on during this time and affirm that there are bigger things in life than the grades we get. Have parents remind students that they and the adult leaders are praying for them.

(Adapted from Group Magazine, May/June 2004)

LETTERS TO A SON AND DAUGHTER

At a meeting for parents, suggest parents write letters to their teenagers. These letters will be put away until the teenager has moved away from home or started a family of his or her own. Here are a few ideas on getting started:

- Make your letters scene-driven. Life is lived in scenes, and it's these scenes that we connect to, just as we connect to scenes in movies that move us or touch us in some way. Therefore, think of an event, and write about what you remember about your kids in that moment, what you saw in them, and how it touched you.
- Make the letters personal and real. Don't be afraid to put your heart on the page.
- Write with variety. Make some of the letters long, some short, and some just fun, and throw in a myriad of writing styles.
- Don't make quantity the goal. It would be great to have 20 or more letters, but a few meaningful letters are more than many young people ever get.
- Have fun with this. You don't have to be a great writer; just write from your heart.
- Keep it a secret. We all like surprises, especially when they've been planned for a long time.

Don't let parents forget to tell their children now all the great things they put in their letters. As parents think about these letters, they'll become more aware of things they want to say to their teenagers in the present. Encourage them to take hold of these opportunities as God gives them in the here and now.

(Adapted from Group Magazine, March/April 2004)

PARENT GROUP

Offer an opportunity for parents to learn from one another in a safe, informal environment with a once-a-month "youth group for parents" that meets at the same time as the youth group.

This is a support group, not a parenting class, but it's best if a skilled facilitator can help your parent group get off the ground. Eventually this role can be passed on to the parents. Here are suggestions from a parent program that's now in its sixth year:

- Begin meetings with a check-in time that allows parents to share key issues and gives them an opportunity to get to know each other better.
- Less structured, more free-flowing discussions provide a less stressful environment and encourage more participation. Parents genuinely enjoy having "downtime."
- Be flexible. The most productive discussions sometimes come from responding to issues that parents bring up during check-in. This might mean dropping the planned topic for the night.
- Avoid debates by reminding everyone that this isn't what the group is about.
- If non-teenager/parent but church-related issues surface, ask for a group consensus about pursuing these topics.
- Avoid discussing serious emotional issues. In these cases, privately suggest that the family pursue professional counseling.
- Open and close with prayer to reinforce the spiritual aspects of parenting.
- Get feedback about how the group is or isn't meeting parents' needs. Ask for suggestions, and change as necessary.

(Adapted from Group Magazine, November/December 2003)

COMMUNICATION CIRCLES

Because the composition of a youth group usually changes from year to year, it can be a challenge to build a sense of community between parents and adult leaders. Here's a discussion-starter exercise that can be used at a parent meeting to begin to create connections.

Have parents and adult leaders form groups of three to five, depending on the overall number of those attending. Begin by identifying one volunteer in each group to go first in the exercise. Next, explain that as you go through a list of fill-in-the-blank statements, you'll respond first and then each group's members will respond within their circle. Have each person take 30 seconds or so to complete the statements.

You can touch on as many topics as you like or target one specific topic. It's helpful to start by sharing surface-level stories and then gradually move into more personal areas. Some possible statements include the following:

- In my free time I enjoy...
- My favorite place I've visited is...
- Something that's old and valuable to me is...
- The first memory I can recall is...
- What I hope to accomplish as a parent/adult leader is...

(Adapted from Group Magazine, September/October 2003)

PARENTING TOOLBOX

Do the parents of the teenagers in your youth group perceive you as a partner? If you'd like a creative way to show that you want to work together as a team, bring along a toolbox and use it as an introduction for your next parent meeting.

Begin by saying that every parent has many useful tools for raising teenagers. Then illustrate your point by holding up various tools and connecting each one to a parenting resource.

For example, pick up a hammer, and remind parents that the Bible is a powerful tool that instructs parents on how to raise children. A screwdriver can represent resources such as books, tapes, and conferences about parenting. Hold up a pair of pliers, and make the connection to teenagers' schools, which offer not only education but also opportunities for involvement in sports and extracurricular activities. Then hold up a wrench, and speak to parents about your desire to be a useful tool in helping them teach and disciple their teenagers.

Conclude by making the point that sometimes we mistakenly rely on one tool to do all the work or grab for the handiest tool, even though it might not be the right one for the job. For example, we might depend on sports and school to do the major work of developing our young people. But if we want to get the job done right, we have to take full advantage of all the tools that God has given us.

(Adapted from Group Magazine, September/October 2003)

HOME DELIVERY

Family ministry is vital to youth ministry, but if you're just starting out, how do you find a way to genuinely connect with your students' families? Here's one way you can create an opening into their lives: Offer to bring dinner into their homes.

Dinner is a great time to connect with family members because it's often the only time they talk to each other. Plus, you take the load off families' busy schedules by delivering dinner.

Reserve an evening in advance for each family. Give family members a few options to choose from (for example, pizza, fried chicken, Chinese takeout, or sandwiches), and take their orders ahead of time.

When you visit a family's home, besides making a point to encourage the family members, observe the way they communicate and interact with each other. This can give you valuable insight into your student's life. If all the family members are Christians, offer to pray with them before you leave. If not, wait and see if God uses your little dinner visit to open some doors.

(Adapted from Group Magazine, May/June 2003)

EXPERT OPINION

When you're looking for ways to affirm the parents of your young people and offer them expertise, don't overlook their potential to help each other. Plan a "parent idea-swap."

Set the date, get the word out, and be present to facilitate the discussion. Establish a clear ground rule that people don't need to agree but everyone does need to respect others. Get conversation started by presenting scenarios about issues that teenagers and parents might be facing, such as dating do's and don'ts or curfew problems. Encourage parents to share their reactions to the scenarios and their real-life experiences.

Help parents understand that the way they've handled a problem in the past may be just what another parent needs to hear right now, especially when setting parameters with his or her teenager.

(Adapted from Group Magazine, May/June 2002)

FAMILY CONNECTION

Pizza's always a good bet for a youth ministry party, especially one that welcomes newcomers to your church. Don't just invite new teenagers, though—invite their families as well.

Several times a year, depending on the size of your church, invite new families to a pizza party hosted by your youth group members, their parents, and your adult volunteers. (You might want to try this at the beginning of the school year, after Christmas holidays, and after Easter.)

This is a great way to connect new students with their peers, new parents to other parents, and everyone to your adult staff. It also gives you an opportunity to tell parents and teenagers about your programs, plans, and vision for youth ministry.

(Adapted from Group Magazine, September/October 2001)

MINISTERING TO NON-CHRISTIAN PARENTS
BY DAVE LIVERMORE

Parents are one of my favorite parts of youth ministry. For those of you who are now questioning my sanity, hear me out. OK, I'll admit that parents have brought me plenty of angst throughout the years, but a turning point happened for me several years ago when I began to see my role as "youth pastor" as not being exclusively to those between the ages of 13 and 18. Instead, I began to see how my calling included ministry to the parents and families of those students in our ministry. I began to feel my heart being tugged for the other people living in the same homes with the students who spent countless hours and weeks with me.

But what about when the parents involved don't share the Christian faith? What's our role in ministering to those parents, and how does that affect how we minister to their teenagers?

Answering a question like that forces us to step back and examine how we view our "missionary challenge" in relation to non-Christian parents. Whether we're ministering to Buddhist parents in Thailand, atheist parents in Los Angeles, or your average, everyday parent in Midwest America, our job is not so much to eradicate Buddhism, atheism, or consumerism. Instead, our number one job is to bless these parents with Christ, giving them a living picture of Jesus.

OK, that sounds like something a seminary guy would say. But what the heck does that mean?!

I think it starts with continuing to do the biggest thing you're already doing—serving kids. Nothing endears someone to me more than when they do something for one of my daughters. Spend time with one of my girls, speak into her life, cheer her on, challenge her, and reinforce the good things happening in her life—anyone who does that has my attention. And I would guess that's exactly what most of us are doing with the kids in our youth ministries.

Granted, not every non-Christian parent is going to welcome a radical Christ-follower spending countless hours with his or her child. But even some of the most antagonistic parents I've encountered still welcome and appreciate the efforts of a caring adult pursuing their teenager. Communication is key. Even if parents don't share the worldview and values we do, they have values nonetheless, and we need to honor and respect those as they "loan" us their children for periods of time.

Of course, if we see our "youth leader" role as including ministry to parents, then we'll also look for tangible ways to minister directly to parents. Expressing care in times of need, rejoicing with them over their victories, and doing all the kinds of things you would do if parents were 15-year-olds in your ministry are the same kinds of ways we can minister to them as 42-year-olds. (And, of course, it probably won't be you doing this personally with all these parents but recruiting others to do it with you!)

In addition, provide these parents with resources on parenting teenagers. Parents of every faith are seeking help on how to survive their job of parenting. Giving parents of all faiths good direction and counsel on how to rear their teenagers is every bit as much the gospel as walking them through your personal testimony. And if you offer parent seminars frequently, it's a great way to connect the non-Christian parents of students in your ministry to the Christian parents. If you're a parent of teenagers yourself, don't be afraid of owning up to your own fears and shortcomings as a parent. There's nothing endearing about being lectured by a "pseudo-Messiah figure" on parenting.

Other than the age-old problem of time, it's not hard for most of us to think about the value of serving non-Christian parents. But if you're like me, giving them a chance to serve us personally becomes much harder. I hate to ask for help, period. Worse yet is having to appear needy to a non-Christian parent. But slowly I'm learning how important it is to let my non-Christian friends give me words of encouragement, lend me a tool, or even "pray" for me.

Find appropriate ways to let non-Christian parents serve in your youth ministry too. I've often tapped these parents to drive vans, collect money at weekend events, share their expertise on a given topic, and cook meals for a weekend outing.

It was while driving down a highway late at night that I talked to Al about what I envisioned life on the new earth would be like. Several times Al unabashedly proclaimed that he didn't think there was any such thing as life after death. But that night, he was captivated by the thought of "what if."

I was stirring the sloppy Joes next to Joan on the weekend camping trip with the high school seniors when she said, "Something in me just feels so alive and whole when I'm with this group of kids. It's different from when I go places with school groups."

It was while setting up chairs in the university room in northern India that Girish, the Hindu father of one of the teenage boys participating in the weekend conference for Christian youth, turned to me and said, "I don't like most Americans. But seeing the sweat roll off your head to set up these chairs shows me you must really believe in what you've been teaching these boys and girls."

I'd love to take credit for having strategized ways to embody Jesus to all these people. But these conversations just happened. I've fumbled over words and lost good opportunities as many times as I've jumped into the moment and said something that triggered a good dialogue. The gospels don't describe Jesus giving countless sales pitches to the people he met. Instead, we read about one unique conversation after another. As Jesus simply encountered people, he reflected his Father's glory through the questions he asked, the way he responded to their pain, and the ways he allowed them to serve him.

And we'd be well-served to empower the Christian teenagers of these non-Christian parents to follow a similar approach. While there's a place for these youth (and us!) to explicitly share that Jesus is Lord and calls for complete surrender and allegiance, the ancient words of Saint Francis of Assisi should be our modus operandi for how we and our students minister to non-Christian parents—"Preach the gospel by all means possible, and if it's really necessary, you could even use words."

If parents are one of my favorite parts of ministry, parents from different faiths probably even trump my love for working with Christian parents. They challenge me, inspire me, and compel me to live out my calling to be an agent of Christ's redemption to all who cross my path—Christian and non-Christian, old and young, Eastern and Western.

Dave Livermore has a heart for the globe and has had the opportunity to serve with national leaders in more than 50 countries. Dave is executive director of the Global Learning Center at GRTS (Grand Rapids Theological Seminary) and is co-founder of Intersect, a ministry that provides leadership training and consulting to emerging leaders in ministries around the world. Dave has authored two books and numerous articles and training manuals. He loves to take deep theological truth and make it profoundly relevant to students and leaders. Dave and Linda Livermore live in Grand Rapids, Michigan, along with their two daughters, Emily and Grace. Some of their favorite family activities include traveling, biking, reading, eating Asian food, and walking to the local ice cream shop—Jersey Junction!

YOUTH GROUP MEETING ACTIVITIES INVOLVING PARENTS

COMMUNICATION SKILLS SEMINAR

This meeting outline presents a plan for a seminar on communication skills. This will provide practical and helpful tips for parents and students to use in communicating with one another.

Before this meeting, read through this meeting plan and acquire a working knowledge of the material presented. Set up your meeting area with two chairs on the stage area (or at the front of the room) and chairs facing the presenting area. The audience chairs should be moveable so they can form groups for small-group discussion.

In preparation for the meeting, read through the skit-starter scenarios on pages 136-137. During the meeting, you'll need to pick volunteers from the audience and guide them through this series of role-plays. Consider which attendees you might choose to have participate. Hopefully your audience will include some parents and teenagers who don't mind hamming it up in front of a crowd. Keep in mind each of these simple role-plays has a specific goal, so your actors must be able to act out the scenario clearly and quickly to accomplish each goal in these impromptu skits.

Make a photocopy of the "Family Discussion Topic List" handout (p. 139) for each person.

You may want to hang a list of questions on the wall in your meeting area so small groups can see them and discuss them at their own pace. If you choose to do so, here are the questions you should list:

- When you are in an intense discussion, how do you communicate physically?
- When you are communicating with someone really well and feel like you have a connection, what is going on around you? How do proximity, eye contact, nonverbal communication, and other elements play a part?
- What factors make you unable to communicate well with someone?

Be sure to make your meeting room inviting and presentable. As people arrive, ask parents and students to sit with their other family members. Say: **Thank you for joining me for this seminar about communication. Communication is a set of skills that take time and effort if we want to get better at them. Nobody is perfect at communicating, and everyone has room for improvement. Practicing these skills is one of the most important things we can do. You have taken a bold and important step in being here. Today we're going to cover some basic but important skills you should be aware of when you're trying to communicate with your teenager or your parent.**

Announce that you will be mediating a series of role-plays that will require volunteers. Ask for two volunteers to act out your first skit.

When you have your two volunteers, secretly share the following scenario with them:

Skit 1: The World's Worst Communicators

In this skit, your volunteers will discuss their recent experiences at the county fair. During their conversation (or two different conversations), they should demonstrate no eye contact, speaking for their own agendas, easy distraction, and utter frustration with one another.

After you give the volunteers their directions, let them ramble for a few minutes. After a few minutes, stop the skit and ask the group the following questions:

- **What did you notice about how the volunteers were communicating?**
- **What worked well?**
- **What did not work at all?**
- **What did you see up here that reminded you of yourself?**
- **Volunteers, is there anything you would like to share about your experience as the participants?**

After your discussion, ask for two more volunteers to act out another skit.

When you have your two volunteers, secretly share the following scenario with them:

Skit 2: Too Much Eye Contact

In this scenario, your volunteers should discuss their favorite foods. Have the volunteers for this skit sit too close to each other and have too much eye contact with one another.

Turn your volunteers loose. Then after a couple of minutes, end the skit and ask the following questions:

- **What went well in this role-play? Why?**
- **What went poorly? Why?**
- **How did the amount of eye contact affect the discussion?**
- **Volunteers, is there anything you would like to share about your experience as the participants?**

After your discussion, ask for two more volunteers to act out another skit.

When you have your two volunteers, secretly share the following scenario with them:

Skit 3: No Eye Contact

Have volunteers discuss their dream vacations. During this conversation, have them sit back-to-back.

Allow your volunteers to act out the skit. Then after a couple of minutes, end the skit and ask the following questions:

- **What was effective in this role-play?**
- **What was ineffective?**
- **How did the lack of eye contact affect the discussion?**
- **Volunteers, is there anything you would like to share about your experience as the participants?**

After your discussion, ask for two more volunteers to act out the last skit.

When you have your two volunteers, secretly share the following scenario with them:

Skit 4: Too Close or Too Far

Have volunteers talk about their jobs or their favorite classes in school. This time have them begin their conversation from across the room. During their discussion, have them slowly walk toward one another until they are nose-to-nose. For extra laughs, allow them to talk nose-to-nose for 30 seconds or even longer before ending the skit.

After the skit, ask the following questions:

- **How did distance affect the conversation?**
- **When was conversation most effective and comfortable?**
- **Volunteers, is there anything you would like to share about your experience as the participants?**

If you hung the questions on the wall before the meeting, point them out to participants.

Say: **Now let's make this a little more personable. Form small groups of five to eight people, and discuss the following questions:**

- When you are in an intense discussion, how do you communicate physically?
- When you are communicating with someone really well and feel like you have a connection, what is going on around you? How do proximity, eye contact, nonverbal communication, and other elements play a part?
- What factors make you unable to communicate well with someone?

Allow small groups several minutes for discussion. Ask volunteers to report what their groups talked about.

Say: **We have just witnessed and discussed a few of many communication skills many people take for granted. In this hectic world, it's rare that parents and students have the opportunity to practice communication skills with one another. That's why we're going to take advantage of the opportunity we have right now. Keep in mind that we're concentrating mostly on skills, not necessarily content. I'll give you a list of topics to discuss with your family while you're practicing these skills.**

Ask family members to join together and find an area where they can have some privacy. Give each family a photocopy of the "Family Discussion Topic List" handout. Instruct families to read through the list together and discuss the topics for 20 minutes. Encourage them to practice effective communication skills as they talk.

After approximately 20 minutes, notify the families that they should wrap up their discussions and come back to the large group.

After the family discussions, ask the following questions:
- **What was surprising about these exercises?**
- **What did you find helpful?**
- **When during the discussion with your family did you feel understood and connected? Why?**
- **What are some communication skills you need to practice?**
- **What are some ideas you can share with others here to make sure better communication skills are practiced in your homes?**

Say: **I admire you for coming to this meeting and participating in this opportunity to develop and practice effective communication skills. As you trust God to help you communicate more effectively, your family will grow in closeness, health, and wisdom. And that is part of God's plan for you.**

Read Ephesians 4:14-16 aloud. Pray aloud, asking God to bless the communication efforts of the families in your church and to give them patience and wisdom in relating to each other. Close by saying: **May your family grow in wisdom and understanding as you honor God by becoming better communicators.**

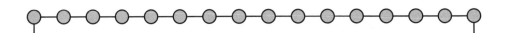

FAMILY DISCUSSION TOPIC LIST

Before you begin your discussion, please read the following guidelines together so everyone in the family can hear and acknowledge these requirements.

We have a chance to practice important communication skills as a family. This time is not a therapy session; however, we may discuss topics that stir up intense emotions and create some tension. For this experience to be successful, we must agree to the following guidelines:

1. I am going to take it slow and allow others to speak their points.
2. I agree that others may disagree with my opinions.
3. I will be quick and concise to get my point across.
4. I know that nobody can disagree with what I am feeling, and I cannot disagree with what other people are feeling (we can only disagree with opinions).
5. If I do not understand what is being said, I will slow the conversation down by asking questions or repeating what I believe someone is saying.

As a family, pick one of the topics below and discuss the topic using appropriate eye contact, nonverbal communication that shows you're really listening, appropriate tone, and the right amount of space between people. Keep in mind the five agreements above.

• A current event that members of the family have differing opinions about
• A religious or philosophical topic that family members may look at differently
• A recent movie or popular song and its impact on culture or family members
• A fear

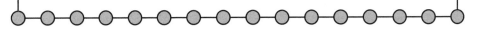

STUDENT APPRECIATION BANQUET

This dress-up event to affirm teenagers will help parents publicly affirm and show affirmation to their kids. The whole event will focus on the positive traits of students and what their parents appreciate about them.

The first thing you'll need to do to prepare for this event is find a nice setting. If your church has a large fellowship hall or other appropriate room, make sure it's free on the evening you have in mind. If not, contact local banquet facilities to book a place. Don't overlook the importance of holding this event in a classy facility. For example, don't host it in your smelly, old-couch, pizza-stained-carpet youth room. You want to send the message that teenagers are important to your church and to their parents. You also want to bring parents and teenagers together in a neutral setting, where neither group will feel like they're in the other's home turf.

Well in advance of this event, send an invitation to each student in your group as well as to his or her parents. Tell them where and when the event will be held. Also make sure they know this will be a dress-up event. (Be sure to specify whether you expect formal, semiformal, or business casual attire. Otherwise people are likely to panic when some show up in tuxedos and others in sweaters.) Be sure to ask that people R.S.V.P. so you know how many (and whom) to plan for. But knowing today's busy families, you'll probably still have to follow up on some of your invitations to find out whether people are coming.

After the invitations go out and you've assembled your guest list, send a follow-up letter only to the parents who are planning to attend. In your letter explain to parents that the purpose of this event is to take advantage of the opportunity to publicly show and tell their kids how important they are and to bless them in a powerful way. Ask them to come prepared to publicly share some words of affirmation, encouragement, and praise for their teenagers.

Also ask parents to give you a few photos of their teenagers that you can use for a slide show. And with your letter, include a form for parents to fill out, describing their kids. For example, your form might include these items:

• Full name:
• Something funny or cute your teenager did as a baby or toddler:
• Your teenager's favorite thing to do at home:
• Something that makes your teenager unique:

Ask parents to give you the pictures and the completed forms a few weeks before the event.

Once you have the pictures and completed forms, use them to put together a slide show. Take the pictures to a photo developer, and request that the pictures be made into slides. Or scan them into a computer, and create a

PowerPoint presentation. Put the slides of the students in alphabetical order, and find someone who will read aloud the forms parents filled out as their teenagers' pictures come up on screen.

Speaking of finding people, you'll also need to find people to help decorate and make food for the event. (Or if you really want to break the bank on this one, hire a caterer.) Make sure the food will be good, but don't get too fancy. Most people don't like fancy food. Pasta dishes are a good idea. Ask your decorating volunteers to make place cards so they can assign seats for all the guests. That way you can make sure families will sit together—that's very important!

About a week before the event, remind students to dress up for the evening (and to show up, if you have a particularly forgetful group). You may even want to call all the parents who have committed to attendance, making sure they'll remember to be there.

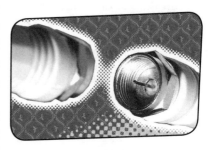

The day of the event, work with your volunteers to decorate the facility. Don't worry about making it look like a wedding reception or prom night. A few simple touches will do the trick. The point is to create a welcoming and celebratory atmosphere and to show everyone who attends that he or she is important. You probably can accomplish this with some streamers, balloons, and a banner.

Before everyone arrives, set up the equipment for your slide show. Make sure everything is in working order and the volume on your sound system will be appropriate. Don't forget to make a microphone available to the person who will be reading student profiles during the slide show. You'll also need a microphone available at the front of the room or onstage so family members can get up and share their affirmations.

As people arrive, let them mingle just a little before serving dinner. As they're eating, welcome everyone and break the ice by having families share stories with each other. You may want to ask a couple of questions like these:

- What is your funniest family vacation story?
- What's the greatest cooking disaster your family has ever known?
- How many pets has your family owned, and what were their names?
- Who in your family is most likely to win a Nobel Prize? Why?
- Who in your family is most likely to end up on a funny home video show? Why?
- If you had to describe your family with a movie title, which movie would you choose, and why?

As you're serving dessert, dim the lights and begin your slide show.

After the slide show, let everyone know the microphone is open for parents to share what they love about their kids. You may be nervous that no one will share (after all, their kids *are* teenagers), but you may be surprised at some of the awesome things parents will have to say. Frankly, the students will be surprised too—and they'll never forget the words they hear. Allow plenty of time for this sharing, and be ready for some emotional moments. And be sure to let students know they're free to share positive words for their parents as well.

At the end of the evening, thank everyone for coming and for sharing his or her positive words. Close in prayer, then encourage families to continue sharing positive words at home. Remind parents that their words can be an incredible blessing to their kids.

As a bonus, videotape this event. Families may want to look back and remember the special moments they shared during this evening.

PERSON HUNT

Small groups of youth make their way through the mall corridors, their eyes peeled for their suspects: Sin-D, Tom the Bomb, and Mrs. "Dirty" Poole. Each suspect's strategy is different. Sin-D stays on the move, casually moving from store to store. Tom the Bomb takes a different approach; in a subtle disguise he sits almost motionless at the fountain and chuckles as the youth walk right by!

That is Person Hunt.

This activity, designed for both youth and their parents, is a fun, creative way to get youth and their parents involved in a youth event. Several parents "hide" in a mall while small groups of youth search for them. The activity has several variations and can also be used in conjunction with a Bible study.

The Planning

1. Plan a day and time for the event. The best time is when a mall is relatively crowded but not totally packed. Early evening usually works well.

2. Contact parents to help with the event. You will need some parents to walk around with the small groups of "hunters" and other parents to be the people being hunted.

3. Take pictures of the parents who will be hunted. Depending on the size of your group and the size of the mall, you will want to keep the number to between three and five. Parents should be instructed to look as inconspicuous as possible on the day of the hunt. They may want to disguise themselves but should do so in a way that would look like a regular mall-goer.

4. Use the pictures to make "Wanted" handouts to give to each group. The kids should not know who is to be hunted prior to the event. For the "Wanted" posters, try to think of fun, criminal-type nicknames for each of your suspects.

5. Make sure you have enough other parents coming so you have at least one adult with each group of searching youth. The youth should be in groups of no more than five.

The Person Hunt

1. On the day of the event, you will want to meet the suspects at the mall *prior* to meeting the youth and at a *different* location from where you will meet the youth.

2. Give each suspect a pen. Suspects will have to sign their names on their wanted posters when they are found by each group. They are *not* to be "captured" or brought back to the starting point by the groups. Once the paper is signed, that group moves on, and the suspect continues to wander for other groups to find.

3. Give the suspects the start time, then go and meet the youth. Once all the youth have arrived at the designated starting point, break them into groups of no more than five, and give each group at least one parent to stay with them. Give each group the list of suspects, and remind them that they are only to get the suspects' signatures, not to capture them.

4. Announce the time they have to find the suspects. You will want to give them one to two hours, depending on the number of suspects they are looking for.

5. Once the groups have returned, reward them with ice cream or some other snack. You may also want to go back to a person's house or even reserve a place at the mall to conduct the debriefing and Bible study below.

Helpful Hints

Here are a few ideas for making the game run smoothly:

1. Keep the department ("anchor") stores off-limits. These stores are so large that finding the suspects can become almost impossible.

2. Make sure the suspects know the time frame of the hunt. They may want to become more "obvious" toward the end of the time period, especially if no student groups have found them.

3. Adults walking with the groups should be instructed to keep the groups on task but not to get too stringent about the students stopping at stores or taking a look at the latest CD. Part of the fun of the game is that they are at

the mall. However, the adults need to make sure the youth do get back to the game and don't just go off to the mall's movie theater!

4. Remember that picture taking and video recording are usually not allowed in malls. So don't try to add this kind of element to the game or to video your youth playing the game.

Debriefing and Bible Study

The Person Hunt works great as a fun outing with youth and their parents. However, you may want to go one step further and end the activity with a short debriefing and Bible study. Both the parents and the youth should be included in the study. If at any time during the discussion either group seems to dominate, you will want to say something like "So what do any of you parents think?" or "Let me hear the thoughts of one of the youth."

Ask:

- **How did you feel as you were searching for the suspects? Did you stay pretty focused, or were you easily distracted?**
- **What were some of the things that distracted you? As the time wore on, did it become harder to keep looking? Why?**
- **Can someone tell us about a time you lost something and took a long time looking for it?**
- **What are some of the feelings we have when we have to find something that we care about?**

Say: **Listen as I read to you a parable that Jesus gives in Luke 15:8-10.** Read the passage.

Ask:

- **What happens to the woman in the story?**
- **What does she do when she finds the coin? Why do you think she does this?**
- **What parallel does Jesus make between the woman in this story and God, whose angels are rejoicing?**
- **Why do you think there is so much rejoicing when one sinner repents?**
- **What picture of God does this parable paint for us? What do we learn about God from it?**
- **In what ways is God always on a "person hunt"?**

Depending on your group, you may want to take some time here to explain the gospel using the language of a "person hunt." The following may serve as a guideline:

Say: **Today we spent time on a person hunt, searching for some people who didn't particularly wish to be found. God does the same thing. He is** portrayed in the Bible not only as a woman looking for a lost coin but also as a shepherd looking for his lost sheep and a father peering down a street looking for his lost son. And sometimes the people God is looking for don't want to be found. But when he finds them—when people understand that God loved them enough to give his own Son to die for them—then God can hardly contain his joy! And it is far more thrilling than the fun you had finding people in the mall. God is finding them for eternity! So has God found you? Or are you still hiding? You know, he loves you and wants to show his grace and forgiveness to you that only come through Jesus. Maybe today is the day he will find you. If you think so, I would love to talk with you about it for a few minutes as soon as we have finished here today.

Ask:

- What are some of our responsibilities once we are found by God?
- In what ways do all of us who are found then begin to participate in the person hunt ourselves?
- Could someone share about the way God found you? Please tell us.

End the debriefing with a time of sharing about different ways God met with the adults and kids in your group. Close in prayer, and be sure to stay visible and available for any youth or adults who might want to talk with you.

MY KID'S CRIB

Cribs is a recently popular MTV show in which celebrities give tours of their luxurious homes. Create your own "My Kid's Crib" night as a special event for your youth and their parents. This event will involve showing videotaped clips of different youth "cribs" and a Bible study that talks about heaven, the ultimate "crib."

The Planning

1. Decide how to advertise the event to your youth. You may want them to know nothing about what is going to happen, so you would tell them only that it is a special youth group event. You may or may not want to even tell them that it is one that involves their parents.

2. Communicate the plan to the parents, asking them to videotape about a minute's worth of their kids' rooms. Tell them not to do any narrating since the idea of the activity will be to try to guess whose room is being shown. However, they may want to focus on some of the unique features of the rooms that would hint at whose rooms they are. Since many parents may not have video or digital video capability, you can also arrange times during the school day to stop into teenagers' homes and take the video clips yourself.

3. Give a clear and early date of when the clips are due back to you, then take some time to put them together, preferably on one CD or tape. As you do this, be sure to keep track of whose room is whose!

4. When the evening of the event comes, set up a projector or TV to show the room clips. Either have the youth just call out whose room they see or ask them to stay quiet and write down each of their guesses to see how many they know.

Hints

1. If your youth group is small enough to get a clip of each person's room, then attempt to do so. However, if your group's size makes this unreasonable, then attempt to get a certain number from each age group so all ages are represented (two rooms of ninth graders, two rooms of 10th graders, and so on).

2. Preview clips and be sensitive to what images you show and which kids might be especially embarrassed. The goal is to have fun and create some suspense as to whose room will be shown. The goal is *not* to show a teenager's underwear pile on the floor and cause him or her great embarrassment.

3. Depending on how computer savvy you are, you may want to ask for the clips to be taken in only a digital format to make cutting and pasting them together much easier.

4. Give parents (or yourself) a lot of time to get the clips recorded and spliced together. Several months may be needed to communicate the idea to parents, get the clips, and get the clips ready for a showing.

The Bible Study

After the clips have been shown and the rooms have been identified, move into a Bible study on heaven, our ultimate crib.

Say: **We have taken some time tonight to look at your cribs—and, wow, we may have seen more than we bargained for!**

Ask:

• **Think about some of the celebrity homes you have seen on different TV shows. What are some of the "perks" you have seen in those homes?**

• **What are your feelings toward these things? Which ones do you think would be the most fun to have?**

Say: **We as Christians have a very special crib that we can look forward to living in for eternity: heaven. Let's look at some of the descriptions of heaven found in Revelation. You should break into groups of five to eight people—some parents and some youth should be in each group.**

Give participants time to get into groups. Once there tell each group to turn to Revelation 21:15–22:6. Ask each group to look over these verses in Revelation and write on paper what heaven looks like. In other words, if groups were to take a picture of what heaven looks like according to this passage, what would they see? Give groups about 10 minutes to jot down their descriptions. (A creative alternative to this activity is to hand out markers or colored pencils to each group and have groups attempt to draw the descriptions they are reading.)

When all groups have finished, have several representatives from each group share some of what they wrote.

Ask:

- **How do you feel when you think about these images?**
- **What about this description strikes you as the most interesting or as the one thing you most look forward to seeing?**
- **How does the description of heaven match the character of God?**

Have everyone turn in the Bible to John 14:1-6. Ask for a volunteer to read the passage aloud.

Ask:

- **What does this passage say about heaven ("Father's house")?**
- **What does this passage say about what Jesus is doing in heaven?**
- **How does this information help us and encourage us as we live our lives in the here and now?**
- **What is the way to get to heaven?**
- **Why is Jesus the only way?**
- **What does it mean for us to live as people who are looking forward to heaven?**

Say: **Today we have seen some of your cribs, and we have also seen a bit about the best crib of all: heaven. But there is only one way to get to this great place of gold and light and truth and happiness—through Jesus Christ. Let's pray together.**

During the prayer you may want to offer an opportunity for youth or parents to commit their lives to Christ so they, too, can go to heaven, to the place Christ will prepare for them. You can also pray that the believers would live in a way that shows their hope and expectation of a life of eternity with God.

WE WERE THERE ONCE

This is a fun and informative way to help parents and teenagers communicate with one another through one of your weekly meetings. By way of preparation, have parents send you pictures of themselves as teenagers in advance. Place these around the room on the walls with blank sheets of paper underneath them.

Activity 1

As everyone enters, invite students to walk around the room and see if they can identify their friends' parents from their teenage pictures posted on the walls. Ask them to write the names of the families underneath the pictures.

Introduce yourself and explain the purpose of your meeting tonight. Tell everyone that you are going to have some fun ways for parents and students to think about what it would be like to be in the other person's shoes. Then they will have a chance to ask each other questions anonymously.

Activity 2

Have a drama in which a teenager and a parent get into an argument. Have a parent play the role of the teenager and a teenager play the role of the parent. The drama could present the same argument from each of two perspectives. It might read as follows:

Parent: (*To the audience*) This is what I heard.

Teenager: Mom/Dad, can I go out tonight?

Parent: Where are you going?

Teenager: Out!

Parent: With whom?

Teenager: People!

Parent: I think we should talk about this.

Teenager: (*With exaggerated anger*) Why do you always have to question my judgment? How come nothing I ever do is good enough for you? You always have to know every little detail of everywhere I go and everything I'm doing. Can you say "micromanagement"? Do you hate me? Here! Here's a leash for you to tie around my neck! Just use it to drag me around wherever you want to go, and I'll just wander along behind you until I'm 40!

Parent: I just wanted you to know I cared.

Teenager: (*To the audience*) But this is what *I* heard.

Parent: Cinderella, did you finish scrubbing the toilets yet?

Teenager: That's not my name, Mom.

Parent: Sorry, I forgot, which one are you again?

Teenager: Can I go out tonight?

Parent: Not likely. Where do you want to go?

Teenager: The movie starts at 7. Rated G. Running time 1 hour, 26 minutes, out for ice cream, approximately 23 minutes, which puts me home at 8:49.

Parent: You forgot driving time. That's it, you're grounded.

Teenager: Why do you always want to know so much?

Parent: Look! Do you know how much trouble teenagers can get in today just by walking outside the door? There are car accidents, kidnappings, school shootings, and bad SAT scores! How do I know what you're into? Are you on drugs? And who are these friends you're going out with? They look shady to me! Shady! And who's this [fill in the name of someone from your youth group] guy you're hanging out with? When I was a child, we never left the house after 3 in the afternoon, and we liked it that way! Because you know what that creates? Healthy families!

Teenager: I just want you to respect me.

Activity 3

Lead a panel discussion, first with teenagers and then with parents. Have a row of chairs in front of the group. Ask four teenagers, two girls and two boys, to fill the chairs. Solicit anonymous questions on index cards from parents. Invite them to ask anything they've always wanted to know about teenagers and teenage life. Allow 10 to 15 minutes of question-and-answer time.

Next, reverse the roles and ask four parents to fill the chairs. Take questions in the same way from students. Spend the same amount of time in this format.

The only ground rules you might want to set are these:

1. The purpose of the questions is to learn, not to embarrass or point fingers.

2. Don't use the names of your family members.

3. Think of everything you've always wanted to ask because now's your chance.

Activity 4

Lead a discussion and give a talk on what contributes to healthy families. Questions to ask could include the following:

- What is one thing you wish all parents/teenagers would know?
- Why do you think there is so much tension between parents and children during the teenage years?
- What would it take for a teenager to demonstrate to his or her parents that he or she is ready for more responsibility?
- What are some of the emotional experiences parents are having while watching their teenagers grow older?

You might want to look at Exodus 20:12 and Ephesians 6:1-4 to study parents' and teenagers' responsibilities to one another.

Activity 5

Supply a list of encouragement ideas, one for parents and one for students. Suggest that they use these at home in the weeks to come. Ideas include the following:

- If your teenager does something wrong, before discussing the consequences, tell him or her about a time you got in trouble as a teenager and what you learned from it.
- Tell your teenager about a specific way in which he or she has changed your life.
- Tell your teenager about one of your most fond memories from his or her childhood.
- Tell your parent something you have learned about him or her this year that you appreciate.
- Tell your parent about something you've seen him or her do that you hope you do when you're a parent.
- Tell your parents about one of your fondest memories of your childhood.

WE NEED EACH OTHER!

The aim of this youth group meeting is to provide a fun evening that helps parents and teenagers appreciate the different gifts, abilities, and knowledge that each of them has.

In 1 Corinthians 12:14-18, Paul taught that we all need each other:

"Now the body is not made up of one part but of many. If the foot should say, 'Because I am not a hand, I do not belong to the body,' it would not for that reason cease to be part of the body. And if the ear should say, 'Because I am not an eye, I do not belong to the body,' it would not for that reason cease to be part of the body. If the whole body were an eye, where would the sense of hearing be? If the whole body were an ear, where would the sense of smell be? But in fact God has arranged the parts in the body, every one of them, just as he wanted them to be."

This meeting outline aims to bring this point home to your teenagers and their parents experientially. You'll find here suggestions for activities that will work best when parents and teenagers work together. Create a program for the evening by picking the activities that you think will work best with the people who will be there. Think about what types of things the parents might excel at and what the teenagers might excel at. Feel free to add your own ideas too. Parents and teenagers will play in teams and get points for different activities. The winning team should be the one in which parents and teenagers have worked best together and have correctly identified each other's strong points. Invite your teenagers and their parents to a fun evening together; there's no need to tell them the aim. If they work it out for themselves, it will be much more meaningful.

Get Into Teams

You'll need one slip of paper for each person present, pens, and two bowls.

At the start of the evening, put the parents and teenagers into mixed teams of six to eight people. Get all the parents to write their names on slips of paper and put them in a bowl. Get all the teenagers to write their names on slips of paper and put them in another bowl. Work out how many teams you need. First, pick a parent for each team from the parents' bowl, and then pick a teenager for each team from the teenagers' bowl. Continue until all the names have been picked. You may need to share any leftover parents and teenagers between teams, but because of the types of activities you'll be doing, as long as the teams have roughly the same number of people, they should be fair.

Music Quiz

You'll need a CD player and/or a tape player, music CDs, a recordable CD or blank tape, pens, and paper.

Before the session, devise a music quiz. You need questions that teenagers will find easy to answer but parents won't have a clue about, and vice versa. So choose current singers, bands, and songs as well as singers, bands, and songs from when the parents were teenagers. Write questions in the following categories:

- Lyrics—Give a line from a song, and ask the teams to sing the next line.
- Introductions—Play the introduction to a song, and ask teams to identify the song before the actual singing starts.
- Members of a band—Give a team the name of a band, and get them to list all its members.
- Bits and pieces—Record snippets of 10 songs—about 10 seconds of each—onto a tape or CD, one after the other. Play the tape or CD, and get the teams to identify the songs; they'll get a point for the singer and a point for the name of the song.

You could ask a parent and a teenager to help you compile the quiz, but of course they won't then be able to participate. Some questions all the teams will be able to answer by writing the answers down; other questions will need to be played in rounds, with a different question directed to each team. Award points for correct answers.

Bashball

You'll need a soccer-sized ball and space to play in.

This game will favor the teenagers because it involves bending over a lot! It can be a fast and furious game, and you need at least eight people to play it. Have people stand in a circle with legs apart so their feet touch those of the players next to them and there is sufficient space for a ball to pass between their legs. Once in this position, players are not allowed to move their feet or legs.

The aim of the game is to stop the ball from going between your legs by bending over at the waist and using your hands. If the ball does go between people's legs, they are "out." They stay in position, though, and stand with their arms folded or on their heads. From now on, if any players accidentally knock the ball through the legs of someone who is out, then they will also be out. The winner is the last person who is "in"! The game starts, and is restarted each time someone is out, by one player throwing the ball to try to get it through someone's legs.

To play the game, ask each team to nominate two or three people to play, depending on how many teams you have. Award points to the last three people who are in—10 points to the winner, 5 to the person who came in second, and 2 to the person who came in third. Add these points to the accumulated total for each team.

Galosh Throwing

You'll need some galoshes; a large hall, parking lot, or field to play in; a tape measure; chalk; and masking tape.

This game will favor the adults, especially the men, because it requires strength! Mark a line at one end of the hall with masking tape. The aim of the game is to throw the galosh the farthest. Ask each team to nominate one or two people to participate. Get participants to take turns throwing the galosh as far as they can. Appoint a judge who will mark with chalk the place where the galosh landed and then measure the distance from the starting line. Again, award points for the top three contestants—10 points for the person who threw the farthest, 5 points for the person who came in second, and 2 for the person who came in third.

Wanted

You'll need computers with a graphics package that your teenagers will know and a printer—access to the Internet is optional.

Give each team the challenge of creating a fun "Wanted!" poster about your church leader. It should have a picture of him or her on it and say what he or she is wanted for and what the reward for capture is. Get them to plan the posters in their teams and then use the computers to design them and print them out. Parents may have more input on the ideas about the poster; teenagers may be more able to use the computers and create a good design. If you have lots of teams and not many computers, run this activity concurrently with the next one so one or two teams can work on their posters while the others are being dramatic! Award points for originality, design, humor, and general "wow" factor.

Video Drama

You'll need a TV, DVD player or VCR, and DVDs or videos.

This is another quiz that you'll need to devise beforehand. In this quiz, teams will watch a video clip and then will need to act out what happens next. You will need to appoint a judge who knows the film clips and can decide how close to the original the acted-out versions are! Like the music quiz, choose some films that parents are likely to know and some films that teenagers are likely to know. If all the teams are playing at the same time, show the clips in a round, giving each team an opportunity to act. If you are doing this at the same time as the design activity, give each team three or four clips to act out one after the other, but make sure the other teams can't oversee what they are doing.

Refreshments

You'll need drinks and cookies.

If some teams aren't active at any one time, let them sit down, have a drink, and talk to each other!

Awards Ceremony

At the end of the evening, have an awards ceremony where you announce the winning team and give those team members a prize. Have smaller prizes for the other teams, too, so everyone gets something. You could ask everyone to say one thing he or she has enjoyed about the evening. You'll probably find that someone makes a comment about appreciating the need to work together; if no one does, you can say how you've enjoyed seeing people working together!

LEARNING FROM EACH OTHER

The aim of this youth group meeting is to help parents and young people understand that they can learn from each other, no matter what their ages and life experience.

Who Taught You That?

You'll need slips of paper, a pen, and a bowl.

Write on slips of paper simple skills that people will have learned as children—for example, tie your shoelaces, ride a bike, play football, read, bake a cake, knit, write your name. Have at least one slip for each person present.

At the start of the session, pass around the bowl. One person at a time will draw a slip and then share with the rest of the group who taught him or her to do that skill and any memories of that person. Other people can chip in with their stories too. Once everyone has drawn a slip, go around the group once more, this time asking people to share the latest thing they learned and who, if anyone, taught them. This activity will help people realize how much they owe to people in the past who have helped and taught them. It will help them reflect on whether they are still learning from others.

Bible Study

You'll need Bibles, paper, and pens.

Split the adults and teenagers into two separate groups. They will each need a space in which to read and discuss, so one group may find it helpful to go into another room. Give the adults the following Bible passages and questions:

- Samuel and Eli, 1 Samuel 3:1-21
- David and Saul, 1 Samuel 17:1-51, especially verses 26-40
- What did the young person have that the adult didn't?
- What might the adult have learned from the young person?
- What have you learned from a young person in the past?
- What might hinder or stop you learning from young people?

Be ready to summarize the stories when the groups get back together.

Give the following passages and questions to the teenagers:

- Elizabeth and Mary, Luke 1:26-45
- Paul and Timothy, Acts 16:1-5; 19:21-22; 1 Timothy 4:11-16
- What did the adult have that the young person needed?
- What might the young person have learned from the adult?
- How have adults helped you in your faith?
- What might hinder or stop you learning from adults?

Be ready to summarize the stories when the groups get back together.

Give the groups 15 minutes to read and discuss the passages. Call them back together, and get each group to give feedback on what they discussed. Make the point that young people are used to learning from adults—they have done it all their lives so far! As they get more independent, they may be tempted to think they know enough now and can do their own thing, but there's always more we can learn from each other. Adults are used to teaching young people, but they also need to be open to learn from young people. Although it's more common for teenagers to learn from adults, these Bible stories show there are times adults can learn deep lessons from young people.

What I'd Like to Learn From You

You'll need two large sheets of paper and pens.

Write "What I'd like to learn from adults" on one sheet of paper and "What

I'd like to learn from teenagers" on the other sheet of paper. Split the adults and young people into two separate groups again, and give each group the appropriate piece of paper and some pens—the adults will be thinking about what they'd like to learn from teenagers, and the teenagers will be thinking about what they'd like to learn from adults. Send them into their separate rooms again, and give them 10 minutes to brainstorm exactly what they'd like to learn from each other and write it on the sheet—not what they think the others would like to teach them, but what they really want to know about.

Gather everyone into the same room again, and get one parent to read what is on the adult sheet, elaborating if necessary. This will enable the comments to remain anonymous. Get the teenagers to respond to what the adults have written. Can they teach those things? How? Then get one teenager to read the comments on the teenager sheet, again adding any detail that's needed. Get the adults to respond to what the teenagers have written. Can they teach those things? How? Encourage families to talk about this exercise when they get home. Encourage everyone to look for opportunities to learn the things they wrote down and maybe to take the initiative in talking to each other.

Giving Thanks

You'll need a piece of thin wire about 5 feet long for each person (florist's wire that is covered in plastic is ideal), wire cutters or strong scissors, and a small standing cross or a candle.

Ask people to reflect for a moment on who has most helped them grow in their faith. It could be someone older or younger than they are. It might be a family member or someone outside the family. It could be someone they have never met but whose books or tapes have been formative. The person may be alive or dead. Give each person a piece of wire, and ask participants to manipulate their wires to spell the names of the people who influenced them. People will effectively write the names in joined-up writing using the wire instead of ink on a page. As they bend their wires, encourage them to think about those people and to thank God for them.

When everyone has finished writing the names, put the cross in the center of the group or light a candle to symbolize Jesus as the light of the world. Invite people one by one to lay their names around the cross or candle, briefly explaining who their people are and how they have been influential. Each person can also pray, thanking God for that person. When everyone has laid down his or her name, encourage people to think about how they in turn can inspire others in their relationship with God. Finish by reading 1 Timothy 4:12, one of the verses the teenagers will have looked at earlier, as an exhortation to encourage others in their faith. You could add the words "or old" as follows: "Don't let anyone look down on you because you are young—or old—but set an example for the believers in speech, in life, in love, in faith and in purity."

LOST AND FOUND

Invite parents to attend a special youth meeting, and enlist their help in an all-out game of Hide-and-Seek. Ideally, this game should be played outside after dusk at a campground or park or in a darkened building.

Meet beforehand with parents, and give each parent a point value between minus 50 and 100. Write these on pieces of paper, and tape them to their backs with the numbers facing in so they can't be seen. Next, ask parents to hide in different places.

Meanwhile, students should be in a separate area. Assign a parent or youth sponsor to keep students occupied with music or silly games until all parents are in place.

When parents are safely in their hiding places, join the teenagers and give them the rules of the game. In teams, they should seek out lost adults and shine flashlights on the adults when they are found. The parents should then accompany that team as they continue their search. The signs on their backs should remain untouched until the very end.

Divide the group into teams of five or six. Each group should be given a flashlight and orders to search for lost parents hiding all over. Be sure to let them know the boundaries of the playing field and any areas that are off-limits. Blow the whistle as you send them on their hunt to let parents know they are on their way.

Blow the whistle again 15 or 20 minutes later to let everyone know it is time to come back together. Even parents who are still hiding should emerge and join the main group. Allow each team to display its finds and add up the point totals it has earned by removing the numbers on each parent's back. (Any negative numbers will be subtracted from the total! Ouch!)

Afterward, consider gathering around a campfire or grill and enjoying s'mores together as you help apply the simple game of Hide-and-Seek to their relationships with God.

Display a box of lost and found items. Together, take a look at some of the items that have been long forgotten. Raise the point that in our state of lost-ness, we are never far from the heart and mind of God.

Explain that we aren't placed on earth accidentally, and even though there are billions of people on the planet, each one of us matters to God. Jesus is on a mission to seek and save each one. Read Luke 19:10 aloud.

Allow a time of sharing in which parents (or teenagers) can share their own experiences of how God found and rescued them.

Even though God wants to be in a relationship with us very much, he doesn't force himself on us. In fact, God wants us to make some effort to find him as well. Ask volunteers to read these Scripture passages aloud: Proverbs 8:17; Jeremiah 29:13; and Acts 17:24-28.

After a time of sharing, ask questions such as "What state were you in when God found you?" "How has your life changed since you are no longer lost but found?" "What efforts are you making to seek God?"

End the evening with a time of prayer thanking God for the great lengths to which he has gone to find and claim us as his children. Seek his heart and will as you silently wait on him.

STUNT DOUBLE NIGHT

Invite parents to your youth meeting for a special "Stunt Double" night. Parents and their teenagers should dress identically. Prepare your classroom in advance with fun Olympic-type decorations, and have small trophy cups, ribbons, or medals that can be awarded to winners of various events.

Plan several comical games in which teams of parents and their teenagers choose which person they think can better represent them. In each instance, either the parent or the teenager will compete with others for ridiculous prizes you have created. Some game ideas might include the following:

- Stumpers—Give a quiz about useless trivia.
- Sock wrestling—Two people try to pull the socks off each other's feet using only their feet.
- Long jump—See who can jump the farthest with an inner tube around his or her waist.
- Feats of strength—Have pairs engage in arm-wrestling contests.
- Gymnastics—See who can do the most graceful cartwheel.

Create ribbons or trophies for the winners, awarding things such as the "Most Likely to Injure Himself and Others Doing a Cartwheel" award, "Knows More About Bad '80s Movies Than Anyone Should" award, and "Monster Feet of Steel" prize. The more absurd, the better.

After a time of fun and games, ask questions such as "What is the purpose of stunt doubles?" "Why are they able to do things an actor or actress is unable to do?" and "Are there people in your life who step in to help with difficult things you can't manage on your own?"

Ask parents to share examples of sacrifices they may have made on behalf of their children.

Use this time of discussion to bring the tone of the meeting from very silly to very serious. Ask everyone to turn in their Bibles to Isaiah 53. Allow volunteers to read portions of the entire passage aloud. While the Scripture is read, consider showing appropriate scenes from the movie *The Passion of the Christ.* Carefully screen the parts you select so there is nothing too graphic or offensive shown—for example, a tormented Christ praying in the garden or on trial before Pilate. Let the clip play without the sound as a mere backdrop to what is being read. The real focus here should be on the Scripture.

Afterward, discuss how Jesus took our place on the cross. He took punishment that was meant for us and managed a task we could have never accomplished on our own—righteousness before God.

Bring the idea of stunt doubles full circle by asking students for real ways they can emulate Christ and resemble him more closely. Together, brainstorm verses in Scripture that urge us to be Christlike. Get things started by reading Philippians 2:5-11 aloud.

Ask questions that challenge parents and teenagers to live their lives differently in the days to come, making a greater effort to be like Jesus out of gratitude for all he has done.

CAREER FAIR

The parents of your students may not agree on everything, but ask who wants their teenagers to become successful adults, and you'll see every hand shoot up.

Every parent wants his or her child to succeed, to make it as an adult.

And while the definition of *success* varies, it usually includes selecting an appropriate career—and taking steps to prepare for it.

You can help, and parents will be grateful for the effort. So grateful, in fact, that they're often willing to *help* you help their kids.

And here's what help looks like: a career fair.

Designing a Career Fair

A career fair is like show and tell for adults. That is, it's a program where adults describe what they do for a living.

To be useful the fair needs to have presentations from Christian adults who work in a wide variety of careers.

Aim to have at least 10 careers represented from across the spectrum of the trades and college-is-required professions. General categories might include agriculture, management, sales, the service sector, transportation, high tech, health care, people-helping professions such as social work and the ministry, and the armed forces. Visit the U.S. Department of Labor's Web site at www.bls.gov to find a comprehensive listing of job categories. Then, with a church directory in hand, think through who in your church works in those job categories.

Start with the parents of your teenagers. Since you want them involved in the career fair program, you'll want to ask them to represent their job categories.

You'll ask adult volunteers to do three things:

1. Prepare a summary sheet for distribution.

Review the sample summary sheet on page 162. It answers the questions your career volunteers are likely to be asked. Using a standard form is critical; it guarantees that teenagers and their parents can easily compare and contrast careers.

Be sure your career volunteers fill out the *entire* form, especially concerning rewards and challenges. Ask volunteers to keep information general. For instance, firefighting might be very rewarding because of the opportunity to help others but challenging because of the need to work night shifts.

2. Be willing to answer questions.

Teenagers and parents may have specific questions about a volunteer's career. Tell volunteers to give answers that are *typical* of the career. If your senior pastor entered ministry only after a misspent youth and two prison terms, that won't be the career path you necessarily want to recommend.

3. Be able to provide one-day job-shadowing opportunities.

This is what makes your career fair so valuable. Teenagers and their parents will be able to not only ask questions but also arrange for teenagers to get a taste of the career in question. That's a *tremendous* benefit.

Be clear that all arrangements must be made between teenagers' parents and the career volunteers. Also, if you use background screening on volunteers in your ministry, either screen the career volunteers or make it clear to parents that these volunteers have *not* been screened.

In your publicity about the career fair, include a list of the careers that will be represented, and consider holding the fair during a regular youth group meeting time. This will not only build attendance but tightly connect this helpful meeting with your youth ministry.

Adapt the following for your meeting:

Before the Meeting

Ask career volunteers to submit completed summary sheets one week before the career fair. Make enough copies of summary sheets to give each teenager a complete set.

Arrange your meeting space so individual career volunteers have room to sit and there are chairs nearby for parents and teenagers who want to discuss careers in detail. Place a poster announcing each career near where the appropriate volunteer will sit. Give all career volunteers name tags.

Serve snacks! Have them available throughout the time parents and teenagers mingle with the career volunteers.

Introduction

Welcome parents and teenagers, and introduce yourself. Share a brief story about an early job you held or how you came to be in your current career. Be light and humorous; your goal is to diffuse any tension parents and their teenagers might be feeling.

Then take no more than 10 minutes to share the following:

Say: **There was a time people didn't have much choice in their careers; whatever their fathers did, they did. The land was passed down, or the tools, and the tradition was carried on.**

Those days are over.

Now teenagers looking into the future have many more options about career choice. But for Christians, some things remain the same no matter where we work: We're in ministry.

The idea that some professions are Christian (missionary, Christian recording artist, youth pastor) and others are secular (homemaker, teacher, police officer) is a flawed notion. According to Scripture, *everything* we do is to be directed by God. We're to glorify God 24/7, and that includes the hours we're at work.

Read 1 Corinthians 10:31 aloud.

Say: **Within some general guidelines, what makes you an effective ambassador of Christ isn't what profession you have but how God uses you through that profession—and how you go about doing your work.**

The careers you see represented here are sacred because the Christians in them have decided to let God use them in their careers.

Before you visit with these people, let me share some career advice that comes straight from Scripture.

Your career isn't all about the money.

Read Mark 8:36-37 aloud.

Say: **The single highest unit of worth in the universe isn't a career that pays six figures. It's you. Jesus came and died for you to redeem you. Don't trade your relationship with him for mere money.**

Read 1 Timothy 6:10 aloud.

Say: **Your career *is* about the money—a little.**

When you work, it enriches your life in some important ways.

Read Titus 3:14 aloud.

Say: **You're able to provide for yourself and not needlessly consume the resources of others. At bare minimum, you can take care of yourself. And living forever in your parents' basement isn't an option no matter how big and** scary supporting yourself might feel. In 2 Thessalonians 3:10, Paul writes, "For even when we were with you, we gave you this rule: 'If a man will not work, he shall not eat.' "

Beyond keeping ourselves fed, work lets us care for our families.

Read 1 Timothy 5:8 aloud.

Say: **Plus, when you work and prosper, you have something to share with others. You can help meet the needs of the poor. You can support those who pastor you. You can contribute.** (Leviticus 19:10; Ephesians 4:28; Galatians 6:6)

When you decide to work—to have a career—you begin to earn money. That money can allow you to do ministry in your own life, the life of your family, and the lives of others around the world.

Success is in the eye of the beholder.

Read Mark 8:36 aloud again.

Say: **If having the latest, greatest toys matters to you because that's how you signal that you're successful, you've settled for second best.**

Who will you stand before at the end of your life? Whose judgment matters most? If you're like me, you want to hear "Well done, good and faithful servant," and I won't hear that if I'm too busy chasing status or prestige or career advancement to serve. Decide now who is *really* your boss and in whose eyes you want to be judged a success.

When selecting a career, determine to be a servant.

That doesn't mean you have to park cars for a living forever. It does mean you need to carve out a career somewhere you can serve God and others.

Meet the physical needs of people. That can happen in a variety of ways, and all of them can be ministry.

Meet the emotional needs of people. Those people may be your customers, your clients, or your colleagues—your co-workers.

Ever and always, meet the spiritual needs of people. Whether you're scrubbing out toilets or scrubbing a chest before performing open-heart surgery, you'll find God puts people in your life who don't know him. How you do your work and what you say when you're with others can introduce them to God.

Share a story from your life about how God used a colleague in a work setting to meet real needs and the impact that had on your life.

Then announce that parents and teenagers will have up to 40 minutes to move from career volunteer to career volunteer. Give a five-minute signal to gather people back together for the closing.

Closing

Use this time as a dedication of your teenagers as they seek careers. Pray for them and the lives that will be touched through their work lives.

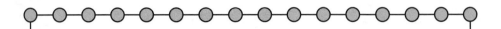

CAREER SUMMARY SHEET

Career: _____

Brief description of typical job duties: _____

Typical starting salary: _____

What skills are needed to be successful in this career?

_____

_____

What training (collegiate and/or on-the-job) is ideal to prepare

for this career? _____

_____

What are typical working conditions like for this career?

_____

_____

What's rewarding about this career?

_____

_____

What's challenging about this career?

_____

_____

How can God use someone who's in this career?

_____

_____

14

PARENT-TEENAGER FAITH CONNECTIONS

The following ideas are taken from "Parent-Teenager Faith Connections" by Group's Youth Ministry Summiteers, which appeared in the July/August 2004 edition of Group Magazine.

PLAN A FUN-FOR-ALL EVENT.

Transform any fun recreational event your kids generally like to attend (going to the amusement park, a concert, and so on) by tapping into the church budget to cover the costs. Announce and advertise that each youth's "price of admission" is to bring a parent to the event. Send information to parents about the event, along with possible faith discussion questions tied to the event so they can prepare to take the lead in intentional interactions with their children.

HOLD A FAMILY MOVIE NIGHT AT CHURCH.

Before the film, have families make a cardboard cutout of their car to watch the movie from. Make sure families sit together, and start the film early enough to have them talk about faith insights and applications using questions you provide. Offer free or low-cost popcorn, snacks, and beverages.

HAVE THE PARENTS WRITE "HONOR LETTERS" TO THEIR TEENAGERS.

Tell them to write specific reasons they're proud of their kids, then share the letters at a special banquet, camping trip, or retreat.

PLAN QUARTERLY PARENT SUPPORT GROUPS.

Send out a survey to your kids' parents with 20 or so parent information or training options, and ask them to pick their top four choices. Then bring in speakers and trainers to address those topics in an interactive way. That means you must make sure it's not straight lecture—parents need to interact with one another.

PUT UP A BULLETIN BOARD JUST FOR PARENTS.

Put together a ministry team of kids who'll be responsible for a bulletin board that chronicles your youth ministry activities with photos, handouts, testimonials, encouraging quotes, and relevant statistics. Place a resource stand nearby with books and videos parents can check out that will build confidence in their role as parents.

SHOW PARENTS AND TEENAGERS HOW TO KEEP A FAMILY JOURNAL.

Ask families to make it a regular practice to spend time together journaling about family activities, decisions, struggles, and joys.

SHOW FAMILIES HOW TO WRITE PERSONAL AND FAMILY CREEDS.

First coach kids and parents in writing a personal creed of their own, then have them get together to write a family creed.

PLAN MOTHER-SON OR FATHER-DAUGHTER MOVIE NIGHTS.

Have parents go to a movie of their kids' choosing. Prepare them with some general discussion questions that will help them discern truths and lies in the film. (If you're a subscriber to our online cultural resource—www.ministryandmedia.com—use its new-release movie section for discussion questions.) Then have them discuss the movie after they see it together.

HAVE FATHERS AND SONS GO SHOPPING FOR VALENTINE'S DAY GIFTS FOR MOMS.

Coach fathers to include their sons in the gift decision. And give fathers discussion questions they can use on the ride home to explore issues of romance and honor with their sons. You could also have sons and daughters help the father or mother plan a surprise anniversary celebration.

EQUIP PARENTS FOR COFFEEHOUSE MUSIC DISCUSSIONS.

Have parents take their children to a music store to buy a CD. Encourage them to stop at a coffee shop after their purchase, and give them discussion questions they can use to explore messages on the CD. (If you're a subscriber to our online cultural resource—www.ministryandmedia.com—use its music section for discussion questions.)

PLAN A MONTHLY SCRAPBOOKING ACTIVITY FOR MOTHERS AND DAUGHTERS.

Organize a themed field trip for mothers and daughters on the first Saturday of the month. Give each mother-daughter set a disposable camera, and tell them to use up the roll on the trip. On the last Saturday of the month, have them come back with their developed pictures and scrapbook together, making pages of their memories. After nine months they'll have a full scrapbook of the year's activities together.

ORGANIZE A FAMILY SERVICE PROJECT EVERY QUARTER.

Choose an organization your church already has a relationship with, such as Habitat for Humanity, a local food bank, or a homeless shelter. Ask what help families could provide, then recruit participants.

HAVE PARENTS TEACH KIDS IMPORTANT (AND NOT-SO-IMPORTANT) LIFE SKILLS.

For example, plan a Barbecue University for fathers and sons. Or have mothers teach both sons and daughters domestic life skills such as how to cook, clean, file, and organize.

SIGN UP PARENTS AND THEIR CHILDREN FOR SPECIAL CLASSES.

Try horseback riding lessons, games such as bridge or chess, snorkeling, golf, fly-fishing, hunter safety, or even ballroom dance.

SET UP PANEL DISCUSSIONS WITH FATHERS/MOTHERS AND SONS/DAUGHTERS.

Prepare discussions on faith-life issues such as curfews, whether church-going is necessary for living your faith, vocational choices, and so on. The panels need not have matching pairs of parents and kids—in fact, it's probably better not to have matching pairs.

GIVE PARENTS DISCUSSION QUESTIONS FOR UPCOMING YOUTH GROUP TOPICS.

Suggest parents use the questions on the ride home from youth group or any time they're transporting their teenagers somewhere. You could also e-mail each family a devotion based on the weekly youth ministry topic.

HAVE KIDS DO CHURCH HISTORY INTERVIEWS.

Have teenagers do video interviews with parents, grandparents, godparents, and family friends on church memories such as baptisms, favorite pastors, favorite church activities, and so on. Then edit the videos into one presentation, and play it for the whole church during a worship service.

FORM MINISTRY TEAMS THAT CONSIST OF A PARENT AND CHILD OR AN ENTIRE FAMILY UNIT.

For example, for Scripture readings in your worship service, have each family member perform a different voice—a "reader's theater" version of the Scripture.

TAKE ADVANTAGE OF TAKE YOUR CHILD TO WORK DAY.

Provide parents with targeted information and questions so they can weave faith discussions into their vocational experience.

ORGANIZE INTERGENERATIONAL HOBBY CLUBS.

Survey parents and kids to find all people interested in hobbies such as model trains, cooking, sewing, model airplanes, photography, scrapbooking, stamp collecting, car repair, or home decorating, to name a few. Find "master" hobbyists—whether parent or teenager—to help lead each club. Many children will be interested in their parents' pursuits, and vice versa. The club setting will help build natural relational "bridges."

GIVE PARENTS AT-HOME DISCUSSION SPARKERS.

You can regularly supply parents with newspaper or magazine articles about teenagers, paired with questions to ask their teenagers (if you're a Group Magazine subscriber, use our In the News section for this).

ORGANIZE A MOTHER-DAUGHTER DISCIPLESHIP GROUP.

Use the book *Mothers & Daughters* by Madeleine L'Engle (Gramercy) as the focus for a monthly mother-daughter date night. Put together a small team of mothers and daughters to help brainstorm monthly fun outings paired with faith discussion questions drawn from the book.

AND A BONUS IDEA! BRING IN PARENTS AND TEENAGERS TO CLEAN UP YOUR CHURCH.

Hold a half-day, on-site workday in which parents and their teenagers work together to complete specific tasks within your church. Specific jobs could be cleaning windows, picking up trash on the church grounds, polishing those old wooden pews, painting a Sunday school room, or cleaning up the youth group area.

EVALUATION FOR
PLUGGING IN PARENTS:
200 WAYS TO INVOLVE PARENTS IN YOUTH MINISTRY

Please help Group Publishing, Inc., continue to provide innovative and useful resources for ministry. Please take a moment to fill out this evaluation and mail or fax it to us. Thanks!

Group Publishing, Inc.
Attention: Product Development
P.O. Box 481
Loveland, CO 80539
Fax: (970) 292-4370

● ● ●

1. As a whole, this book has been (circle one)
   not very helpful   *very helpful*
   1   2   3   4   5   6   7   8   9   10

2. The best things about this book:

3. Ways this book could be improved:

4. Things I will change because of this book:

5. Other books I'd like to see Group publish in the future:

6. Would you be interested in field-testing future Group products and giving us your feedback? If so, please fill in the information below:

Name_____

Church Name _____

Denomination _____ Church Size _____

Church Address _____

City _____ State _____ ZIP _____

Church Phone_____

E-mail _____